# THE ENTREPRENEUR'S MINDSET:
# Cultivating Success from Within

By Thomas Moore

# SUMMARY

# INTRODUCTION

"The Entrepreneur's Mindset: Cultivating Success from Within" is not just a book - it is a journey, an exploration of the cognitive landscape of successful entrepreneurs, an expedition into the heart of business success. It is an invitation for you, dear reader, to embark on a transformative voyage that will not only guide you through the uncharted waters of entrepreneurship but also cultivate a mindset conducive to personal growth and success.

The entrepreneurial journey is often romanticized as an expedition filled with triumphs, when, in reality, it is more like sailing on a tempestuous sea. The waves of challenges are high, the winds of change unpredictable, and the shores of success are often elusive. Yet, those who navigate these waters successfully share a common trait: the right mindset.

An entrepreneurial mindset is more than just a state of mind; it is an amalgamation of qualities, habits, and attitudes that sets successful entrepreneurs apart. It encompasses the audacity to dream big, the passion to turn those dreams into reality, the resilience to weather the storm, and the perseverance to keep sailing even when the destination seems far away.

In this book, we will explore the key elements of the entrepreneurial mindset, beginning with the birth of an idea and the discovery of your entrepreneurial spirit. You will understand the power of passion as the driving force of success and learn how visionary thinking can help you see beyond the now.

We will discuss how embracing failure can become a source of profound learning and how resilience can fortify you to bounce back stronger. You will delve into the art of leadership and influencing others, discover how innovativeness can keep you ahead of change, and understand the importance of calculated risk-taking.

Further, the book sheds light on the significance of emotional intelligence in business, the power of persistence, and the necessity of making informed decisions. We will explore the language of business – finance and the power of networking. We will also address the importance of maintaining an ethical business to build trust and reputation.

Finally, we will tackle perhaps the most crucial yet most overlooked aspect of entrepreneurship: life-work balance. It's an integral part of the entrepreneurial journey that impacts not just business success but also personal well-being and happiness.

Each chapter is designed to provide practical insights and actionable strategies that you can implement immediately. Through real-life examples, engaging exercises, and thought-provoking questions, we aim to not only provide information but also inspire introspection and action.

Whether you are an aspiring entrepreneur, a business enthusiast, or anyone seeking personal and professional growth, this book is for you. The entrepreneurial mindset is not confined to the realm of business; it can be applied to all aspects of life.

So, welcome to "The Entrepreneur's Mindset: Cultivating Success from Within." Let's begin this fascinating journey of learning, growth, and success. Because success is not just about reaching the destination; it's also about enjoying the voyage.

# CHAPTER 1: THE BIRTH OF AN IDEA: FINDING YOUR ENTREPRENEURIAL SPIRIT

Welcome to the genesis of your entrepreneurial journey - the birth of an idea and the awakening of your entrepreneurial spirit. This first chapter serves as the starting point, the launchpad from which you'll propel yourself into the dynamic world of entrepreneurship.

Entrepreneurship often begins as a single spark, an idea that ignites the fire of creativity and innovation within an individual. It could be a solution to a persistent problem, a novel way to meet an unfulfilled need, or simply a better approach to something that already exists. It's a moment of epiphany, a flash of insight that holds the potential to change not just an individual's life but also the lives of others.

However, an idea, no matter how groundbreaking, is only the beginning. It's like a seed that, while containing the blueprint of a full-fledged tree within it, requires the right environment and care to grow and thrive. The seed of an entrepreneurial idea needs the nurturing environment of the right mindset – the entrepreneurial spirit.

But what is this entrepreneurial spirit, and how can one find it within oneself? It's not a trait exclusive to a chosen few; rather, it's a potent mixture of passion, curiosity, and determination that lies within all of us, waiting to be tapped into. It is about having the audacity to think differently, the courage to step outside of your comfort zone, and the drive to make your vision a reality.

In this chapter, we will explore how you can ignite the spark of an idea and awaken your entrepreneurial spirit. We will delve into the processes of idea generation and validation, discuss the power of curiosity and observation, and talk about recognizing the potential in everyday experiences.

Whether you already have a business idea that you're excited to bring to life or you're still in search of that initial spark, this chapter is for you. It aims to set you on the path of entrepreneurial thinking, encouraging you to see the world through the lens of possibility and opportunity. It's about finding that spark and fueling it into a flame that lights up your entrepreneurial journey.

So, let's set sail on this exciting adventure, starting at the very beginning – the birth of an idea and the discovery of your entrepreneurial spirit.

## *Sparking the Idea*

There's something magical about the moment when an idea strikes - a spark in the mind that has the potential to start a roaring fire of innovation and success. Yet, despite popular belief, ideas don't usually spring from nothing; they are often the result of a process, a collision of thoughts, observations, and experiences that culminate in a moment of insight.

So, how does one ignite this spark and generate ideas? Here are a few strategies:

### 1. Embrace Curiosity

Every great idea begins with a question. What if? Why not? How can this be improved? Curiosity is the wick that lights the candle of creativity. To spark an idea, you must first foster a sense of curiosity about the world around you. Question everything and seek answers relentlessly.

### 2. Stay Observant

The world around you is filled with inspiration. By honing your observational skills, you can pick up on trends, recognize patterns, and identify problems that need solving. You might discover that the next big idea is right in front of you, hidden in the mundanity of everyday life.

### 3. Learn Continuously

The more you know, the more connections you can make. Never stop learning and expose yourself to a broad range of knowledge. Dabble in different disciplines, read extensively, and cultivate a diverse network of connections. The convergence of different fields often results in the most innovative ideas.

### 4. Brainstorm Freely

Allow your mind to wander, explore, and experiment without the constraints of practicality or feasibility. This process can be solitary or collaborative, structured or free-flowing, but it should always be non-judgmental. Remember, there are no bad ideas in a brainstorming session. It's the quantity that matters more initially, and the quality can be refined later.

### 5. Harness the Power of Daydreaming

Daydreaming often has a bad reputation, but it can be a powerful tool for idea generation. It allows your mind to roam freely, linking unrelated concepts, envisioning possibilities, and conjuring up innovative solutions.

Generating ideas is the first step on your entrepreneurial journey, the spark that lights the path toward building something meaningful and impactful. But remember, an idea is just the beginning. What matters is what you do with that idea and how you bring it to life.

In the next section, we will discuss how to recognize and evaluate the potential of an idea. The goal is to turn the spark into a flame, a fleeting thought into a viable business concept that could change the world or, at the very least, make a corner of it a little better.

Embrace the process, celebrate the journey, and remember - every great achievement started with an idea, a tiny spark in the mind of someone who dared to think differently. And there's no reason that someone can't be you. So, keep questioning, keep observing, keep learning, keep brainstorming, and keep daydreaming. Let the sparks fly!

## Recognizing Potential

Once the spark of an idea has been ignited, the next crucial step on your entrepreneurial journey is to recognize its potential. An idea, no matter how innovative or unique, must have viability and relevance to blossom into a successful venture. But how does one determine the potential of an idea? Here are some strategies to guide you:

**Identify a Need or Problem:** The most successful businesses often stem from solutions to real-world problems or fulfill unmet needs. Ask yourself, does your idea provide a solution to a problem or fulfill a need that isn't currently being met? If the answer is yes, then your idea might have real potential.

**Market Research:** The market provides crucial information about the potential of your idea. Understand your target audience, their needs, and wants. Look at current market trends and future predictions. Identify potential competitors and understand their strengths and weaknesses. Extensive market research can provide valuable insights into the potential of your idea.

**Scalability and Profitability:** For an idea to be successful, it must be scalable and profitable. Can your idea be expanded easily to cater to a larger audience? Can it generate a sustainable profit in the long run? If the answers are positive, your idea may have genuine potential.

**Feasibility:** Consider the feasibility of your idea. Do you have the resources and capabilities required to execute it? If not, can they be acquired? Feasibility is a vital factor that influences the potential of an idea.

**Differentiation:** Does your idea offer something different from what's already available in the market? Differentiation can come in various forms: a unique product or service, a novel business model, a new market segment, or even a distinctive brand personality.

Recognizing potential is about being able to envision the journey of your idea from its current stage to a successful business. It involves critical thinking, comprehensive research, and a clear understanding of your capabilities and resources. It's about looking at the bigger picture and seeing where your idea fits into it.

While it's essential to believe in your idea, it's equally important to approach it with a realistic mindset. Not every idea will have the potential for success, and that's okay. The key is to keep generating new ideas and learning from each experience. Your entrepreneurial journey is not a straight path but a winding road full of learning and growth.

In the next section, we will discuss how to take your potential-filled idea and convert it into a feasible plan. It's about turning potential into action, laying down the blueprint for your entrepreneurial venture.

Remember, the potential of an idea doesn't just lie in its originality or innovation. It lies in its capacity to create value, meet a need, and make a difference. As Thomas Edison once said, "The value of an idea lies in the use of it." So, recognize the potential of your idea and start using it to create something meaningful.

## Feeding Your Curiosity

Curiosity is the fuel that feeds the entrepreneurial spirit. It's the driving force behind innovation, a catalyst for learning and discovery, and a gateway to new possibilities. Entrepreneurs are inherently curious individuals, constantly questioning the status quo, seeking novel solutions, and exploring uncharted territories. But how can you cultivate and feed this sense of curiosity? Here are some strategies:

### 1. Embrace a Beginner's Mindset

Approach the world with the openness and wonder of a beginner. Admit that you don't have all the answers and be willing to learn from every experience. The more you know, the more you realize you don't know, and this fuels the desire to learn more.

### 2. Ask Questions

Practice the art of inquiry. Question everything - why things are the way they are, how they can be improved, and what possibilities lie ahead. Every question you ask can lead to new insights and ideas.

### 3. Read Widely and Diversely

Expose yourself to a broad range of ideas, disciplines, and perspectives. Read books, articles, blogs, and research papers. The more diverse your reading, the more connections your mind can make, leading to innovative ideas.

### 4. Cultivate Diverse Relationships

Surround yourself with people from different backgrounds, industries, and fields of expertise. Engage in meaningful conversations, exchange ideas, and learn from their experiences and viewpoints.

### 5. Embrace Expériences

Step outside of your comfort zone and embrace new experiences. Travel, try new activities, learn new skills, or explore different cultures. Each new experience offers a fresh perspective and feeds your curiosity.

### 6. Reflect and Meditate

Spend time alone in quiet reflection or meditation. This allows your mind to process information, make connections, and generate insights, fueling your curiosity and creativity.

Feeding your curiosity is about cultivating an insatiable appetite for learning and a relentless pursuit of knowledge. It's about embracing the unknown, seeking out the new, and finding joy in discovery.

In the following section, we will explore how to channel this curiosity into action, translating ideas into reality. After all, the true power of curiosity lies not just in asking questions but in seeking answers, not just in dreams but in doing.

As Albert Einstein once said, "I have no special talent. I am only passionately curious." So, feed your curiosity, and let it guide you on your entrepreneurial journey. From this spark of curiosity, your entrepreneurial spirit is ignited, and from there, the journey toward success truly begins.

# The Power of Observation

Observation is one of the most potent tools in the entrepreneur's toolkit. It's the art of consciously watching the world around you with a critical and analytical eye, looking for patterns, trends, problems, and opportunities. Entrepreneurs with keen observational skills often find inspiration in the most unexpected places and are better equipped to adapt to changes and overcome challenges. So, how can you harness the power of observation?

**Mindfulness:** Be present in the moment. When you're fully engaged with your surroundings, you're more likely to notice the small details that others might miss. Mindfulness enhances your observational skills by heightening your awareness of the world around you.

**Active Listening:** Observation isn't just about what we see; it's also about what we hear. By actively listening, you can pick up on underlying messages, detect nuances, and gain insights that might otherwise go unnoticed.

**Empathy:** To truly understand the needs and wants of your target audience, you must be able to put yourself in their shoes. Empathy allows you to see the world from others' perspectives, enhancing your ability to observe and understand their experiences.

**Analytical Thinking:** Observing is not just about collecting information; it's about interpreting that information in a meaningful way. By thinking analytically, you can identify patterns, draw conclusions, and generate insights from your observations.

**Documentation:** Keep a record of your observations. This could be a journal, a digital document, or even voice memos. Documenting your observations allows you to reflect on them later and can serve as a valuable resource for idea generation.

**Being Open-minded:** Observation requires an open mind. Be willing to challenge your assumptions and embrace new perspectives. An open mind allows you to see opportunities where others see obstacles.

Observation is a skill that can be cultivated with practice. It involves being present, listening actively, empathizing with others, thinking analytically, documenting insights, and maintaining an open mind. By harnessing the power of observation, you can uncover opportunities for innovation, gain a deeper understanding of your market, and make more informed decisions.

In the next section, we will delve into how to use these observational insights to define your vision and chart your entrepreneurial path. Remember, the power of observation lies not just in seeing what everyone else sees but in understanding what everyone else overlooks.

So, observe, interpret, learn, and innovate. Let the power of observation guide you on your entrepreneurial journey, illuminating the path to success with insights and opportunities.

# CHAPTER 2: HARNESSING PASSION: DRIVING FORCE OF SUCCESS

Entrepreneurship is often likened to a roller coaster ride - filled with thrilling highs, terrifying lows, unexpected twists, and numerous challenges. It requires immense dedication, unwavering perseverance, and an enormous amount of hard work. But what fuels an entrepreneur through this tumultuous journey? What keeps them going despite the odds? The answer is Passion.

Passion is the fuel that powers the entrepreneurial engine. It's an intense, enthusiastic love for what you do. It's the internal fire that ignites the entrepreneurial spirit, compelling entrepreneurs to pursue their dreams relentlessly, even in the face of adversity.

In this chapter, "Harnessing Passion: Driving Force of Success," we delve into the profound role that passion plays in entrepreneurial success. Passion is more than just a fleeting emotion; it's a driving force that can be harnessed to propel you forward on your entrepreneurial journey. It's the resilient backbone that holds you upright when the ride gets tough and the powerful motivator that pushes you to keep striving for excellence.

This chapter will explore how to ignite, maintain, and channel your passion toward your entrepreneurial venture. We'll discuss how to identify your passion, how it contributes to resilience and perseverance, and how it can be used to inspire others. We'll also address the challenges associated with passion, such as the risk of burnout, and offer strategies to balance passion with pragmatism.

Passion, when harnessed correctly, can transform an ordinary idea into an extraordinary venture. It breathes life into your entrepreneurial dreams and empowers you to turn those dreams into reality. So, let's embark on this exciting journey and discover how to harness your passion as the driving force of your entrepreneurial success. After all, as the famous quote by Steve Jobs goes, "The only way to do great work is to love what you do." So, let's explore how to love your work and let it drive you to greatness.

## Identifying Your Passion

Passion is the foundation upon which the edifice of entrepreneurship is built. It is the force that propels entrepreneurs through obstacles, fuels their determination, and inspires their creativity. However, before passion can be harnessed and directed toward a venture, it must first be identified. But how does one go about identifying their passion? Here are some strategies:

**Reflect on Your Interests and Experiences:** Spend some time reflecting on your interests, hobbies, and past experiences. What activities do you find most fulfilling? When do you lose track of time? What tasks do you look forward to? Your passion often lies in the activities that bring you joy and satisfaction.

**Identify Your Strengths:** What are you naturally good at? Your strengths can be a signpost toward your passion. Often, when we excel at something, we enjoy it more and, in turn, develop a passion for it.

**Look for a Cause:** What issues or causes do you feel strongly about? Your passion might be linked to a cause or issue that you want to address or contribute to. Many entrepreneurs are driven by the desire to make a positive impact on the world.

**Seek Feedback:** Ask for input from people who know you well. They might provide valuable insights about your skills, talents, and interests that you might overlook.

**Experiment and Explore:** Sometimes, the best way to discover your passion is through exploration and experimentation. Try out different activities, take up new hobbies, learn new skills, or venture into different fields.

Identifying your passion can take time and introspection. It's not always a straightforward process, and that's okay. The key is to stay open, curious, and willing to explore. Remember, your passion is something that excites you, energizes you, and gives you a sense of purpose. It's something that you love doing so much that you would do it even if you weren't paid for it.

Once you've identified your passion, the next step is to integrate it into your entrepreneurial venture. In the following section, we will discuss how to translate this passion into a business idea and utilize it as a driving force toward your success.

Remember, as Howard Thurman beautifully put it, "Don't ask yourself what the world needs. Ask yourself what makes you come alive, and go do that, because what the world needs is people who have come alive." So, find what makes you come alive and let that passion guide your entrepreneurial journey.

## Passion vs. Obsession: The Fine Line

Passion and obsession can appear similar on the surface - both involve intense focus, deep interest, and significant time investment. However, the two are distinct in critical ways, and understanding this difference is vital for an entrepreneur's mental health and business success. This sub-chapter aims to draw a clear line between passion and obsession, helping you stay on the healthy side of this fine line.

Passion is a positive, energizing force. It is a love for what you do and a desire to spend time engaging in it. Passionate entrepreneurs are driven by a sense of purpose and fulfillment. They are deeply connected to their work but maintain a healthy balance with other life aspects - relationships, health, hobbies, and personal development.

On the other hand, obsession is an unhealthy fixation. An obsessed entrepreneur is consumed by their work to the point where it begins to negatively impact other areas of their life. They may neglect their health, personal relationships, and self-development, or disregard ethical considerations. Obsession can lead to burnout, isolation, and poor decision-making.

Here are some key differences:

1. Flexibility vs. Rigidity: Passionate entrepreneurs are flexible. They are committed to their vision but open to new ideas and willing to pivot when necessary. Obsessed entrepreneurs, in contrast, are rigid. They may cling to their ideas stubbornly, disregarding valuable feedback or market realities.

2. Balance vs. Neglect: Passion allows for balance. Entrepreneurs passionate about their work can still make time for family, friends, and self-care. However, obsessed entrepreneurs often neglect these areas, resulting in burnout and strained relationships.

3. Motivation: Passion is intrinsically motivated. Entrepreneurs are driven by a love for what they do and the satisfaction it brings. Obsession is often fueled by extrinsic factors like fame, wealth, or the desire to prove oneself, which can lead to unhappiness if these goals are not met.

4. Resilience vs. Fragility: Passionate entrepreneurs are resilient. They see failures as learning opportunities and are not easily discouraged. In contrast, obsessed entrepreneurs may be fragile, with their self-worth tied to their venture's success. Setbacks can lead to severe emotional distress.

Recognizing the difference between passion and obsession is crucial for entrepreneurs. It's important to be deeply committed and driven, but not at the expense of your well-being or ethical standards. In the next section, we will discuss strategies to keep your passion healthy, prevent it from turning into an obsession, and maintain a balanced approach to entrepreneurship. Remember, the goal is not just to build a successful business but to lead a fulfilling, well-rounded life.

## Channeling Passion into Productivity

Once you have identified your passion and recognized the fine line between passion and obsession, the next challenge is to channel your passion into productivity. This involves translating your enthusiasm and energy into tangible results that drive your business forward. Here's how you can achieve this:

### 1. Set Clear Goals

Define what success looks like for you and your business. Your passion can motivate you to reach these goals, but without clear objectives, it can be easy to lose focus and drift off course. Set both short-term and long-term goals and make sure they are Specific, Measurable, Achievable, Relevant, and Time-bound (SMART).

### 2. Plan Your Time

Passion can lead to productivity, but not without a structure in place. Time management is crucial. Develop a daily, weekly, and monthly schedule that allocates time for work, rest, and personal activities. Use productivity tools and techniques, such as the Pomodoro Technique or Eisenhower Matrix, to help manage your time more effectively.

### 3. Stay Organized

Keep your workspace and your work processes organized. This reduces friction and makes it easier to focus on tasks that matter. Use digital tools to manage your tasks, keep track of your progress, and stay organized.

### 4. Maintain Your Energy

Passion is an energy source, but even the most passionate entrepreneurs can burn out without proper self-care. Make sure you are eating well, exercising regularly, getting enough sleep, and taking breaks when needed. Remember, you can't pour from an empty cup!

5. Keep Learning

Use your passion as a catalyst for continuous learning. Stay updated with the latest trends in your industry, learn new skills, and seek out opportunities for growth and development. This not only helps you stay competitive but also fuels your passion and keeps it alive.

6. Celebrate Progress

Recognize and celebrate your achievements, no matter how small. This boosts morale, fosters a positive mindset, and provides a sense of satisfaction that fuels your passion and productivity.

Channeling your passion into productivity is not about working longer hours or pushing yourself to the limit. It's about working smarter, not harder. It's about setting clear goals, managing your time effectively, staying organized, taking care of your physical and mental well-being, continuing to learn and grow, and celebrating your progress.

By channeling your passion into productivity, you can transform your enthusiasm into tangible outcomes, driving your business forward and paving the way for entrepreneurial success. In the following section, we will explore how to use your passion to inspire others and foster a passionate culture within your organization.

# Sustaining the Fire Within

The passion that ignited your entrepreneurial journey is not a finite resource, but it requires careful maintenance to keep it burning brightly. Keeping your passion alive is vital for the long-term sustainability and success of your entrepreneurial venture. Here are strategies to sustain the entrepreneurial fire within:

### 1. Embrace Lifelong Learning

One of the best ways to sustain your passion is to commit to lifelong learning. By continuously acquiring new knowledge and skills, you not only remain competitive in your field but also keep your passion alive by feeding your curiosity and sense of accomplishment.

### 2. Stay Connected to Your 'Why'

Over time, the daily grind of running a business can make it easy to lose sight of why you started in the first place. Regularly reconnect with your 'why'. This could be a desire to make a difference, solve a problem, or express your creativity. Your 'why' will continue to fuel your passion and guide you through challenges.

### 3. Nurture Your Well-being

Passion can wane when you're constantly stressed or burned out. Regular self-care, including proper nutrition, exercise, adequate sleep, and mindfulness practices, can help maintain your overall well-being and keep your passion alive.

### 4. Create a Supportive Network

Surround yourself with people who understand and support

your journey. This could be fellow entrepreneurs, mentors, or supportive friends and family. They can provide motivation, encouragement, and advice to help sustain your passion.

### 5. Celebrate Small Wins

Running a business is a marathon, not a sprint. Regularly celebrating small victories along the way can provide a much-needed boost of motivation and a reminder of the progress you're making, both of which can help sustain your passion.

### 6. Be Open to Evolution

Your passions might evolve, and that's okay. Be open to this evolution. You might find new interests or discover that your passion lies in a different aspect of your business. Embrace this change and let it guide your journey.

Keeping the fire of passion burning is crucial for the long-term success of any entrepreneur. It requires regular fuel in the form of continuous learning, connection with your purpose, self-care, social support, recognition of progress, and openness to change. By sustaining this fire, you'll find the energy, motivation, and resilience you need to persevere in your entrepreneurial journey, even in the face of challenges. As Vincent Van Gogh once said, "What would life be if we had no courage to attempt anything?" So, keep the fire alive and dare to bring your entrepreneurial dreams to life.

# CHAPTER 3:
# VISIONARY THINKING:
# SEEING BEYOND
# THE NOW

Great entrepreneurs do more than just identify opportunities or solve problems of today. They are visionary thinkers who look beyond the present moment, anticipating future trends, challenges, and needs. Their foresight empowers them to create innovative solutions and shape the future, rather than simply reacting to it.

In this chapter, we delve into the art and science of visionary thinking – an essential component of an entrepreneur's mindset. Visionary thinking is what differentiates a business that merely survives from one that thrives and leads. It involves more than just predicting the future; it's about creating it.

The ability to see beyond the now is not a mystical gift bestowed upon a select few. Rather, it's a skill that can be nurtured and developed. In this chapter, we'll uncover the aspects of visionary thinking, such as developing a compelling vision, setting strategic goals, staying ahead of market trends, and fostering an environment that encourages innovation.

As an entrepreneur, your vision serves as the guiding star for your venture. It provides direction, inspires your team, and builds confidence among your investors and customers. It's the big picture of what you aspire to achieve and the impact you want to make. But how do you develop such a vision? And once you have it, how do you translate it into reality?

This chapter will help you explore these questions and equip you with the tools and strategies you need to become a visionary leader. By the end of this chapter, you'll have a clear understanding of how to think beyond the now, anticipate the future, and lead your business toward long-term success.

# The Art of Forecasting

Forecasting is a critical skill for any entrepreneur aiming to stay ahead of the curve and shape their business's future. It involves making educated predictions about what will happen in the future based on data, trends, and insights. While it may seem like a daunting task, particularly in rapidly changing industries, it's an art that can be mastered with practice and the right approach.

Here's how you can refine your forecasting abilities:

**Understand Your Industry:** The first step toward effective forecasting is gaining a comprehensive understanding of your industry. Familiarize yourself with its history, current landscape, key players, and recent trends. This knowledge will form the base from which you can make educated predictions.

**Analyze Trends and Patterns:** Look for trends and patterns within your industry and the broader market. This could be technological advancements, changing customer behaviors, evolving regulations, or new business models. Analyzing these trends can help you predict how they might evolve and impact your business.

**Leverage Data:** Use both qualitative and quantitative data to inform your forecasts. This could be sales data, customer feedback, market research, or industry reports. Data analytics tools can help you make sense of large datasets and draw meaningful insights.

**Keep an Eye on the Broader Environment:** External factors like economic conditions, political climate, societal changes, and environmental issues can significantly impact your business. Stay informed about these broader trends and incorporate them into your forecasts.

**Learn from the Past:** While forecasting is about the future, there's much to learn from the past. Past trends, successes, and failures can provide valuable insights and help you make more accurate predictions.

**Embrace Uncertainty:** The future is inherently uncertain, and no forecast can be 100% accurate. The goal of forecasting is not to predict the future with certainty but to make the best possible guess based on the information available. Be ready to adapt your forecasts as new information comes in.

**Use Scenario Planning:** Given the uncertainty of the future, it can be helpful to consider multiple possible scenarios. Scenario planning involves creating and analyzing several plausible future scenarios, helping you prepare for a range of outcomes.

Mastering the art of forecasting involves a mix of data analysis, trend spotting, intuition, and learning from the past. It requires keeping a finger on the pulse of your industry and the broader environment, continually learning, and being adaptable. By honing these skills, you can better anticipate future trends and challenges, allowing you to make proactive decisions and stay ahead in the entrepreneurial game.

So, are you ready to look beyond the horizon and shape the future? Let's embark on this journey of visionary thinking together.

## The Power of Creativity

In the entrepreneurial world, creativity is more than an advantage; it's a necessity. It is the driving force behind innovation and the engine that keeps businesses moving forward. Visionary thinkers are, above all, creative individuals who see potential where others do not and are not afraid to think outside the box to bring their visions to life.

Here's how you can tap into the power of creativity:

### 1. Foster a Curious Mindset

A curious mind is a creative mind. Cultivate a genuine curiosity about the world, your industry, and people. Ask questions, seek answers, and don't be afraid to dive deep into topics that fascinate you. This sense of wonder can open up new ideas and perspectives.

### 2. Embrace Diverse Experiences and Viewpoints

Diversity fuels creativity. Encourage different perspectives within your team, engage with people from diverse backgrounds, and expose yourself to a variety of experiences. This broadens your viewpoint and fosters creative thinking.

### 3. Make Time for Reflection

Creative insights often come from periods of quiet reflection. Make time for solitude and introspection, allowing your mind to wander and make new connections.

### 4. Encourage Idea Generation

Promote a culture where generating ideas is encouraged, and all suggestions are welcomed and valued. Techniques like brainstorming or mind mapping can help stimulate creative thinking.

### 5. Embrace Risk and Failure

Do not be afraid of taking risks or making mistakes. Often, the most innovative ideas are born from failure and the lessons learned from these experiences.

### 6. Keep Learning

Continuous learning feeds creativity. Always seek new knowledge, learn new skills, and stay up-to-date with the latest trends and technologies.

### 7. Stay Open-Minded

Be open to change and new ideas, no matter how outlandish they may initially seem. Sometimes, the most unconventional ideas can lead to the greatest innovations.

Creativity is not an inherent trait; it's a skill that can be developed and enhanced. By fostering a curious mindset, embracing diversity, making time for reflection, encouraging idea generation, learning from failures, continuously learning, and staying open-minded, you can unlock the power of creativity. This will enable you to see beyond the current reality, envision new possibilities, and bring innovative solutions to life, propelling your entrepreneurial journey forward.

## Embracing Futuristic Thinking

At its core, futuristic thinking involves looking ahead, envisioning the possible futures, and preparing for them today. This forward-thinking mindset is what allows visionary entrepreneurs to anticipate changes, create innovative solutions, and navigate their businesses toward a successful future.

Here's how you can embrace futuristic thinking:

**Develop a Long-Term Vision:** Futuristic thinking starts with developing a long-term vision for your business. This vision should articulate your aspirations and the impact you wish to make in the future. It acts as a guiding star that directs your strategic decisions and helps align your team's efforts.

**Consider Future Trends and Scenarios:** Regularly monitor and analyze trends in your industry and the broader environment. Consider how these trends could evolve and what implications they could have for your business. Scenario planning can be a useful tool for exploring multiple future scenarios and their potential impacts.

**Seek Diverse Perspectives:** Engage with a variety of people to gain different perspectives on the future. This could include customers, industry experts, futurists, and team members from various backgrounds. Diverse perspectives can enrich your understanding of the future and spark innovative ideas.

**Invest in Innovation:** Embrace a culture of innovation. Encourage the generation of new ideas, support risk-taking, and reward creativity. Investing in research and development, staying abreast of technological advancements, and cultivating an innovative culture can position your business at the forefront of change.

**Adopt a Growth Mindset:** A growth mindset is fundamental to futuristic thinking. View challenges as opportunities for growth, embrace learning, and see failure as a stepping stone toward success. This mindset fosters resilience and adaptability, enabling you to navigate the uncertainty of the future.

**Create Future-Ready Strategies:** Translate your understanding of the future into strategic action plans. These strategies should be flexible enough to adapt to changing circumstances and robust enough to guide your business toward your vision.

Embracing futuristic thinking doesn't mean you can predict the future with absolute certainty. It's about equipping yourself with the best possible understanding of what could come, enabling you to navigate the waves of change rather than being swept away by them. By embracing futuristic thinking, you can lead your business toward a prosperous future and make a lasting impact.

## Envisioning Success

Every entrepreneurial journey begins with a vision of success. This vision serves as a roadmap, guiding entrepreneurs toward their goals and helping them make strategic decisions. It motivates, inspires, and fuels their passion, giving them the resilience to overcome challenges and continue moving forward.

Envisioning success involves more than just setting goals. It's about creating a vivid mental image of what success looks like for you and your business. Here's how you can create your vision of success:

### 1. Define What Success Means to You

Success looks different to everyone. For some, it might be financial prosperity, for others, it might be making a positive impact on society, and for others, it might be achieving a balance between work and personal life. Take some time to reflect on what success truly means to you.

### 2. Set Clear, Achievable Goals

Once you've defined what success means to you, set clear, measurable, and achievable goals. These should align with your definition of success and act as milestones on your entrepreneurial journey.

### 3. Visualize Your Success

Visualization is a powerful tool for manifesting your goals. Regularly take time to visualize your success. Imagine how it would feel, what it would look like, and what it would mean for you and your business. This mental imagery can motivate you and make your goals feel more attainable.

4.  Develop a Strategic Plan

Turn your vision of success into a strategic plan. This plan should outline the steps you need to take, the resources you need to gather, and the milestones you need to reach to achieve your vision.

5.  Align Your Team with Your Vision

Communicate your vision of success to your team. Ensure they understand it, believe in it, and see how their work contributes to it. Their buy-in and effort are crucial for turning your vision into reality.

6.  Stay Focused and Resilient

Stay focused on your vision, even when faced with challenges or setbacks. Maintain your resilience and remind yourself of why you embarked on this entrepreneurial journey in the first place.

Remember, the journey toward success is not a straight path. It's filled with twists and turns, ups and downs, successes and failures. But with a clear vision of success, a strategic plan, a committed team, focus, and resilience, you can navigate this journey and make your vision a reality. So, dream big, visualize your success, and embark on your entrepreneurial journey with confidence and determination.

# CHAPTER 4:
# EMBRACING FAILURE:
# LESSONS FROM
# THE DOWNFALLS

As aspiring entrepreneurs, the thought of failure can be daunting. It can stir up feelings of anxiety, fear, and self-doubt. We often view failure as an end, a pitfall that signifies that our entrepreneurial journey has been derailed. However, this perception of failure is one of the most significant obstacles to success. The reality is that failure is not an end, but a beginning - a learning experience that can propel us toward success if embraced and understood correctly.

In this chapter, "Embracing Failure: Lessons from the Downfalls," we aim to shift your perspective on failure and demonstrate how it can be a stepping stone toward success. We will explore the importance of failing forward and using these experiences as lessons to grow stronger and smarter. We will delve into the stories of successful entrepreneurs who have faced their share of failures and used them to fuel their eventual success.

Failure is an inherent part of the entrepreneurial journey. It's a sign that you're pushing boundaries, taking risks, and striving toward your vision, which are all key components of success. By the end of this chapter, you'll understand why failure should not be feared or avoided but embraced as a valuable teacher and guide on your path to entrepreneurial success. This transformative perspective will empower you to face challenges with courage, learn from your mistakes, and persist toward your vision, no matter the obstacles that come your way.

## Redefining Failure

Redefining failure is the first step toward embracing it. It's about shifting your perception from viewing failure as a disastrous end to seeing it as a beneficial stepping stone. Here's how you can redefine failure in your entrepreneurial journey:

### 1. Understand Failure as a Learning Opportunity

Every failure comes with its share of lessons. Whether it's a failed product launch, a rejected proposal, or a business venture that didn't take off, each failure teaches you something valuable about your business, your market, and yourself. Embrace these lessons and use them to strengthen your strategy and avoid similar mistakes in the future.

### 2. Recognize Failure as an Indicator of Effort and Courage

Failure is an inherent part of trying something new and stepping out of your comfort zone. If you're not failing, you're probably not pushing your boundaries enough. Recognize failure as a sign of your effort and courage, and not as a reflection of your worth or abilities.

### 3. See Failure as a Catalyst for Innovation

Many successful products and services we see today were born out of failure. Think of failure as an opportunity to reassess, rethink, and innovate. It challenges you to come up with creative solutions and paves the way for innovation.

### 4. Treat Failure as a Part of Your Growth Journey

Every failure brings you one step closer to success. It's a part of your growth journey, shaping you into a wiser, stronger, and more resilient entrepreneur.

5. Normalize Failure

Failure is normal and common in the entrepreneurial world. Even the most successful entrepreneurs have faced failures. Normalize failure in your entrepreneurial culture, encourage risk-taking, and make it safe to fail.

6. Detach Your Self-Worth from Failure

Your failures do not define you. Detach your self-worth from your failures and view them objectively as external events that have valuable lessons to teach.

Redefining failure involves a significant mindset shift. It requires patience, persistence, and a lot of self-compassion. But once you manage to redefine failure, you'll realize that it's not something to be feared or avoided. Instead, it's a powerful tool that can guide you toward your entrepreneurial success. So, the next time you face failure, embrace it, learn from it, and let it fuel your journey to success.

## Learning from Mistakes

Mistakes are the pillars of learning in the journey of entrepreneurship. They are the unwanted but necessary stepping stones that lead to wisdom and growth. It's through mistakes that we often gain the most valuable insights and skills. Here's how you can effectively learn from your mistakes:

**Acknowledge and Accept Your Mistakes:** The first step to learning from mistakes is acknowledging them. This might seem simple, but it's often the hardest part. It's uncomfortable to admit when we're wrong, but it's essential for learning and growth.

**Analyze Your Mistakes:** Once you've acknowledged your mistake, the next step is to analyze it. What led to the mistake? Was it a lack of information, poor planning, miscommunication, or something else? Understanding the root cause of your mistake can help you avoid similar mistakes in the future.

**Identify Lessons and Create an Action Plan:** Every mistake has a lesson to teach. Identify what you can learn from your mistake and create an action plan to apply these lessons. This might involve acquiring new skills, improving your processes, strengthening your communication, or adjusting your strategy.

**Implement Changes:** Once you have an action plan, the next step is to implement the changes. This might involve taking small steps toward improving, continuously assessing your progress, and making adjustments along the way.

**Share Your Learnings:** Mistakes and the lessons learned from them are not only valuable to you but also others in your team or network. Share your learnings openly. It can help others avoid similar mistakes and create a culture where it's safe to make mistakes and learn from them.

**Forgive Yourself and Move Forward:** Once you've learned from your mistake, forgive yourself. Mistakes are a part of being human and a part of the entrepreneurial journey. Don't dwell on your mistakes or let them hold you back. Use them as fuel to propel you forward.

Remember, making mistakes is not the problem, failing to learn from them is. By acknowledging your mistakes, analyzing them, identifying lessons, implementing changes, and forgiving yourself, you can turn your mistakes into opportunities for learning and growth. This learning mindset will not only help you navigate your entrepreneurial journey more effectively but also empower you to turn setbacks into comebacks.

## From Failure to Improvement: The Process

Turning failure into improvement is a process that requires introspection, resilience, and action. It's about transforming the disappointment of failure into the fuel for growth and development. This process can be broken down into several key steps:

1. Understanding the Failure: The first step in this process is understanding the failure. What went wrong? Why did it go wrong? Analyzing the failure from every angle will give you a clearer picture of what led to the failure and what can be done to prevent it from happening again.

2. Accepting Responsibility: It's important to accept responsibility for your part in the failure. This doesn't mean blaming yourself, but rather acknowledging that you had a role in the outcome. This can be a difficult step, but it's crucial for growth.

3. Learning the Lessons: Every failure comes with its own set of lessons. Identifying these lessons is a key step in transforming failure into improvement. What can you learn from this failure? How can you use this knowledge to better yourself and your business?

4. Creating a Plan of Action: Once you've identified the lessons from your failure, the next step is creating a plan of action. This should involve strategies for avoiding similar failures in the future, as well as steps toward improving your skills, processes, or products.

5. Implementing the Changes: After creating your plan of action, it's time to put it into practice. This could involve implementing new strategies, developing new skills, or making changes to your products or services.

6. Monitoring the Results: After implementing your changes, it's important to monitor the results. Are your changes leading to improvements? If not, what further adjustments need to be made?

7. Celebrating Progress: Remember to celebrate your progress, no matter how small. Turning failure into improvement is no small feat, and every step forward is worth acknowledging and celebrating.

This process is not a one-time event, but a continuous cycle. As an entrepreneur, you'll likely face failures multiple times throughout your journey. But with each failure, you have the opportunity to improve and grow. By understanding, accepting, learning, planning, implementing, monitoring, and celebrating, you can turn every failure into a step toward your ultimate success.

## Accepting and Overcoming Setbacks

Setbacks are inevitable in the journey of entrepreneurship. They are unplanned events that delay or obstruct progress. However, it's not the setback itself that defines us, but how we respond to it. Accepting and overcoming setbacks is a crucial aspect of entrepreneurial resilience. Here's how you can tackle setbacks effectively:

**Acknowledge the Setback:** Before you can overcome a setback, you must first acknowledge it. This means accepting the reality of the situation without minimizing it or letting it overwhelm you. Acknowledging a setback can be difficult, but it's the first step toward overcoming it.

**Give Yourself Time to Process:** It's natural to feel disappointed, frustrated, or upset when you encounter a setback. Allow yourself to experience these emotions without judgment. Giving yourself time to process can help you approach the setback with a clearer mind and more balanced emotions.

**Evaluate the Situation:** Once you've given yourself time to process, the next step is to evaluate the situation. What led to the setback? What could you have done differently? By assessing the situation objectively, you can gain valuable insights into what went wrong and how to avoid similar setbacks in the future.

**Formulate a Plan:** After evaluating the situation, formulate a plan to overcome the setback. This might involve addressing the issues that led to the setback, adjusting your strategy, or developing new skills.

**Take Action:** With a plan in place, it's time to take action. Implement your plan, step by step. Remember, progress might be slow, but as long as you're moving forward, you're on the right track.

**Stay Resilient:** Overcoming setbacks requires resilience. Stay focused on your vision and remind yourself of why you started in the first place. Use setbacks as opportunities to grow stronger and more resilient.

**Seek Support:** Don't hesitate to seek support when overcoming setbacks. This can be from a mentor, a colleague, or a supportive community of entrepreneurs. Sometimes, a fresh perspective or some encouraging words can make all the difference.

Remember, setbacks are not a sign of failure, but a part of the journey. By acknowledging, processing, evaluating, planning, acting, staying resilient, and seeking support, you can not only overcome setbacks but also turn them into stepping stones toward your entrepreneurial success.

# CHAPTER 5: RESILIENCE: BOUNCING BACK STRONGER

Welcome to Chapter 5, "Resilience: Bouncing Back Stronger." This chapter focuses on a core characteristic of successful entrepreneurs - resilience. Resilience, in essence, is the ability to recover quickly from difficulties, bounce back after setbacks, and adapt well in the face of adversity.

Resilience doesn't mean not experiencing difficulty or distress, but rather, it involves responding to these challenges in a way that allows for growth and perseverance. It's about having the mental and emotional strength to navigate through tough times and come out on the other side stronger and more capable.

In the world of entrepreneurship, resilience is essential. The journey of an entrepreneur is filled with challenges, obstacles, and failures. Market dynamics change, competitors emerge, strategies fail, and sometimes, despite our best efforts, our ventures can fall short. It's resilience that enables entrepreneurs to get back on their feet and keep pushing forward, undeterred by these difficulties.

In this chapter, we'll delve into the concept of resilience in more depth, exploring how it empowers entrepreneurs to thrive amidst adversity. We'll explore strategies to build and enhance resilience, discuss the role of a positive mindset, and understand how resilient entrepreneurs turn their failures into opportunities for growth and learning.

Whether you're an aspiring entrepreneur or already on your entrepreneurial journey, this chapter will equip you with the understanding and tools to build your resilience, enabling you to weather the inevitable storms of entrepreneurship and bounce back stronger. As we go through the chapter, you'll gain insight into how resilience can be the key to not just surviving, but truly thriving in your entrepreneurial journey. Let's dive in.

# Understanding Resilience

Resilience, in its simplest form, is our ability to bounce back from adversities. It is a psychological trait that allows us to recover from setbacks, adapt to change, and keep going in the face of hardship. However, resilience is more than just enduring; it is about harnessing the tough times to foster growth and improvement.

To understand resilience, we first need to debunk the myth that resilience is a rare ability only possessed by a few. Resilience is not a trait that people either have or do not have. It's not a fixed attribute, but a dynamic process that involves effort and engagement. Everyone has the capacity for resilience; it just manifests differently in each person.

A second myth about resilience is that it's about toughing it out alone. In reality, resilience often involves seeking help and leaning on others for support. The most resilient individuals recognize their need for help and are not afraid to ask for it.

So, what makes someone resilient?

Firstly, resilient individuals are realistic. They have a clear understanding of their situation and the challenges that lie ahead. They don't downplay their difficulties, but they don't let them be overwhelming either.

Secondly, resilient people have a positive attitude. They tend to view problems as temporary obstacles rather than insurmountable hurdles. They believe in their abilities to overcome these obstacles and are hopeful about the future.

Thirdly, resilient individuals are proactive. They don't wait for problems to go away; they take steps to resolve them. They are solution-oriented and focus on what they can do rather than on what they can't.

Finally, resilient people learn from their experiences. They see failures and mistakes as opportunities for learning and growth. They take the lessons learned from these experiences and use them to build stronger foundations for the future.

In the context of entrepreneurship, understanding and building resilience is fundamental. Entrepreneurs face a multitude of challenges - from financial difficulties to competition, from market uncertainty to personal stress. It is resilience that empowers them to navigate these challenges, bounce back from failures, and continue moving forward. As we delve deeper into this chapter, we will explore how you can build and strengthen your resilience, setting yourself up for long-term entrepreneurial success.

# The Art of Adaptability

The art of adaptability is a critical aspect of resilience, especially in the ever-changing landscape of entrepreneurship. As an entrepreneur, you must adapt to new circumstances, overcome unexpected obstacles, and pivot when your initial strategies don't yield the desired results. Without adaptability, resilience remains incomplete.

Adaptability is about flexibility and versatility. It's about being open to change and ready to shift your perspective and approach based on the demands of a situation. An adaptable entrepreneur is not stuck on a single path; they explore multiple avenues, makes adjustments on the fly, and can transition seamlessly between tasks and strategies.

So, how can you enhance your adaptability? Here are some strategies:

**Embrace a Growth Mindset:** A growth mindset, a concept developed by psychologist Carol Dweck refers to the belief that your abilities and intelligence can be developed through dedication, hard work, and feedback. With a growth mindset, you see challenges as opportunities to learn and grow, rather than threats to your competence.

**Cultivate Curiosity:** Curiosity fuels adaptability. By being curious, you open yourself to new experiences and ideas, increasing your ability to adapt to unfamiliar situations. Make it a habit to ask questions, seek out new knowledge, and challenge your assumptions.

**Practice Problem-Solving:** Enhance your problem-solving skills. Every time you solve a problem, you are essentially adapting to a situation that didn't go as planned. The more problems you solve, the better you get at thinking on your feet and making quick, effective decisions.

**Be Open to Feedback:** Feedback is a powerful tool for adaptation. It gives you a fresh perspective on your work and reveals areas where you can improve. Don't shy away from feedback; seek it actively and use it constructively.

**Stay Informed:** Stay updated with industry trends, market changes, and emerging technologies. This will help you anticipate changes and adapt your strategies proactively.

**Embrace Failure:** Don't be afraid of failure. Instead, see it as a part of the journey. Each failure brings valuable lessons that can help you adapt and improve.

By mastering the art of adaptability, you empower yourself to navigate the unpredictable waters of entrepreneurship. Remember, it's not the strongest or the most intelligent who will survive, but those who can best manage change. As Charles Darwin said, "It is not the strongest of the species that survives, nor the most intelligent; it is the one most adaptable to change." Be that entrepreneur who thrives in change by mastering the art of adaptability.

## Persistence: The Companion of Resilience

Persistence is an entrepreneur's steadfast companion on the road to resilience. The entrepreneurial journey is fraught with challenges - setbacks, roadblocks, failures. But the hallmark of a resilient entrepreneur is the ability to persist through these challenges and to continue pursuing their vision despite the obstacles that stand in their way.

Persistence is a mindset, a way of approaching problems and setbacks with determination and tenacity. It's about not giving up when things get tough, but instead pushing harder, learning from the failures, and adapting your strategies to overcome them. It's about staying committed to your goals, even when progress seems slow, or the end seems far away.

So, how can you cultivate persistence? Here are some strategies:

**Set Clear Goals:** Clear, concrete goals give you something to strive for and can keep you motivated during tough times. Make sure your goals are challenging but achievable, and break them down into smaller, manageable steps.

**Believe in Yourself:** Self-belief is the fuel of persistence. You have to believe in your abilities, in your vision, and in your capacity to achieve your goals. When faced with setbacks, remind yourself of your strengths, your accomplishments, and your passion for what you're doing.

**Embrace Challenges:** Challenges are not roadblocks; they're stepping stones to success. Each challenge is an opportunity to learn, grow, and improve. When you embrace challenges, you become more resilient and more capable of overcoming future obstacles.

**Stay Positive:** Maintaining a positive attitude can help you stay persistent. Positive thinking can boost your motivation, increase your resilience, and give you the strength to keep going when things get tough.

**Seek Support:** Don't hesitate to seek support when you need it. Friends, family, mentors, or peers can provide valuable advice, encouragement, and a fresh perspective. Remember, persistence doesn't mean going it alone; it means staying committed to your journey, with the help of others.

**Celebrate Small Wins:** Celebrating small wins along the way can boost your morale and keep you motivated. Each small win is a step toward your larger goal and a testament to your persistence.

Persistence, coupled with resilience, is the key to long-term entrepreneurial success. As the renowned inventor Thomas Edison once said, "Our greatest weakness lies in giving up. The most certain way to succeed is always to try just one more time." Cultivate persistence, embrace resilience, and keep pushing forward on your entrepreneurial journey.

# *Building Mental Toughness*

Mental toughness is the glue that holds resilience and persistence together. It's the mental grit that allows entrepreneurs to withstand and overcome adversities. It's the ability to remain calm under pressure, manage your emotions, and maintain confidence and optimism despite setbacks or failures.

Mental toughness is an umbrella term that includes a range of traits, including emotional intelligence, self-confidence, positive thinking, and stress management. It is these traits that enable entrepreneurs to navigate the highs and lows of the entrepreneurial journey, making mental toughness an essential part of the resilience toolbox.

### 1. Cultivate Emotional Intelligence

Emotional intelligence involves understanding and managing your own emotions, as well as recognizing and responding to the emotions of others. By cultivating emotional intelligence, you can improve your ability to handle stress, make decisions, and interact effectively with others.

### 2. Build Self-Confidence

Confidence is a powerful motivator. When you believe in yourself, you're more likely to take risks, overcome setbacks, and pursue your goals with determination. Build your self-confidence by setting and achieving small goals, celebrating your accomplishments, and surrounding yourself with positive influences.

### 3. Practice Positive Thinking

Positive thinking can help you maintain your focus and

motivation, even in the face of adversity. Try to maintain a positive outlook, focus on solutions rather than problems, and see challenges as opportunities rather than obstacles.

### 4. Learn Stress Management Techniques

Stress is a part of the entrepreneurial journey, but it's how you manage that stress that matters. Techniques such as meditation, mindfulness, deep breathing, and regular physical exercise can help you manage stress and maintain your mental well-being.

### 5. Embrace Failure

To build mental toughness, you need to change your relationship with failure. Instead of viewing failure as a setback, see it as a learning opportunity. This shift in perspective can help you bounce back from failures more quickly and with greater determination.

### 6. Seek Support

Building mental toughness doesn't mean going it alone. Seek support from mentors, peers, or professional coaches who can provide guidance, encouragement, and a fresh perspective.

By building mental toughness, you equip yourself with the strength and resilience needed to navigate the challenging journey of entrepreneurship. As the saying goes, "Tough times never last, but tough people do." Cultivate mental toughness, and you'll be well-equipped to weather any storm that comes your way on your entrepreneurial journey.

# CHAPTER 6: LEADERSHIP: THE ART OF INFLUENCING OTHERS

Leadership is a cornerstone of entrepreneurial success. It's a bridge connecting your vision to your team, the spark that ignites creativity, and the compass guiding you toward a common goal. Leadership, however, isn't simply about managing or supervising; it's about inspiring, motivating, and positively influencing those around you.

The role of a leader extends beyond the confines of an organization. It impacts the industry, community, and sometimes, the entire world. As an entrepreneur, your leadership style can define your business's culture, determine its course, and shape its future.

This chapter, "Leadership: The Art of Influencing Others," delves into the essential aspects of entrepreneurial leadership. It seeks to equip you with the knowledge and tools you need to become a more effective, influential, and inspirational leader.

We will explore the various facets of leadership, from setting a compelling vision and building a team around it, to fostering a positive and productive work culture. We'll look at how to communicate effectively, how to motivate and inspire your team, and how to navigate the challenges that come with being a leader.

The road to leadership is a journey of self-discovery and growth. It is about understanding your strengths and weaknesses, learning to leverage your unique skills and qualities, and continually striving to improve. It requires patience, perseverance, and an open mind.

By the end of this chapter, you will gain a deeper understanding of what it means to be a leader, what qualities make a great leader, and how you can develop these leadership traits in your entrepreneurial journey. You will discover that leadership, like entrepreneurship, is not merely about financial gains or business success, but about making a difference, influencing positive change, and leaving a lasting impact. So, let's embark on this journey to hone your leadership skills and enhance your entrepreneurial potential.

# Defining Effective Leadership

Effective leadership is a nuanced concept that goes beyond the traditional notion of simply being in charge. It's a dynamic and complex process that involves guiding, inspiring, and influencing others toward achieving common goals.

While the specifics of effective leadership may vary across different contexts and cultures, several key attributes universally define a successful leader. These include the ability to articulate a compelling vision, inspire and motivate others, foster a culture of collaboration and innovation, and make sound decisions under pressure.

Let's delve deeper into these attributes:

**Vision:** A successful leader has a clear, compelling vision and can articulate it in a way that inspires others. The vision provides a roadmap for the future, giving direction and purpose to the team's efforts.

**Motivation and Inspiration:** An effective leader motivates and inspires team members to perform their best. They foster an environment that encourages personal growth and recognizes individual contributions.

**Empathy and Emotional Intelligence:** Effective leaders demonstrate empathy and have high emotional intelligence. They understand and manage their emotions and the emotions of others, allowing them to build strong relationships and navigate complex social situations.

**Decision-Making:** Leaders are often faced with difficult decisions. The ability to make sound, timely decisions— even under pressure or in uncertain situations—is a critical leadership skill.

**Integrity:** Effective leaders model integrity. They are honest, transparent, and consistent in their actions and decisions, which helps build trust within the team.

**Resilience:** Leaders need to demonstrate resilience, the ability to bounce back from setbacks and failures. Resilient leaders use these experiences to learn, grow, and become stronger.

**Adaptability:** In a rapidly changing business environment, adaptability is crucial. Effective leaders are flexible and agile, able to adjust their strategies as needed to meet evolving circumstances.

Understanding these attributes is the first step in your journey toward effective leadership. In the following sections, we will explore how you can develop these skills and apply them in your entrepreneurial journey. Remember, leadership isn't a destination but a journey of continuous learning and growth.

## Cultivating Influence

Influence is the heart of leadership. It's the capacity to shape perspectives, sway decisions, and guide others toward a common goal. It's about creating a positive impact and inspiring change, not through authority or coercion, but through respect and trust. Cultivating influence, therefore, is a critical skill for entrepreneurs aiming to lead successful businesses.

Here's how you can cultivate influence:

1. **Build Trust**: Trust is the foundation of influence. Be reliable, keep your promises, and demonstrate consistency in your words and actions. Show integrity by being honest and transparent, even when it's challenging to do so.

2. **Communicate Effectively**: Great leaders are great communicators. They articulate their ideas clearly and listen actively. They use stories and analogies to make their messages more relatable and inspiring.

3. **Show Empathy**: Empathy enables you to understand others' perspectives and emotions. It allows you to build strong connections and demonstrate that you value and respect your team members.

4. **Lead by Example**: Your actions speak louder than words. Show your commitment to your vision and values through your actions. Your team members are more likely to follow your lead when they see you living up to your expectations.

5. **Encourage Participation**: Encourage team members to share their ideas and opinions. This not only makes them feel valued and involved but also provides them with diverse perspectives.

6. **Inspire and Motivate**: Find out what motivates

your team members and create an environment that stimulates those motivators. Celebrate their achievements, recognize their efforts, and show them how their work contributes to the overall vision.

7. **Provide Mentorship**: Share your knowledge and experience with your team. Guide them in their professional growth and help them navigate challenges. This not only helps them develop but also strengthens your relationship with them.

Influence is not about manipulating others to do your bidding, but about inspiring them to willingly and enthusiastically contribute to a shared vision. By cultivating influence, you can lead more effectively, foster a more engaged and productive team, and drive your business toward success.

Empowering your team is a crucial aspect of effective leadership. It involves creating an environment where each team member feels valued, capable, and motivated to contribute their best to the team's goals. Empowerment boosts morale fosters a sense of ownership and encourages creativity and innovation.

**Delegate Responsibility:** Delegation is not just about distributing tasks; it's about entrusting responsibility. By delegating, you show your team that you trust their abilities and judgment. This not only frees up your time for strategic tasks but also allows your team members to develop their skills.

**Promote Autonomy:** Allow your team members the freedom to make decisions within their scope of work. Autonomy encourages initiative and creativity and helps team members feel more engaged and committed to their work.

**Provide the Necessary Tools and Resources:** Ensure your team has access to the tools, resources, and training they need to perform their jobs effectively. This also includes creating a supportive and conducive work environment.

**Encourage Learning and Development:** Promote a culture of continuous learning. Encourage your team members to develop new skills and provide opportunities for professional growth. This not only helps them in their personal development but also benefits your business in the long run.

**Acknowledge and Appreciate:** Recognition and appreciation play a vital role in empowerment. Acknowledge your team members' efforts and achievements and show appreciation for their contributions. This boosts their morale and motivation.

**Foster Open Communication:** Encourage open and honest communication. Allow your team members to voice their ideas, concerns, and suggestions. This makes them feel heard and valued and can provide you with valuable insights.

**Encourage Team Collaboration:** Promote a collaborative work culture. Encourage team members to work together, leverage each other's strengths, and learn from each other. This fosters a sense of community and mutual support.

Empowering your team creates a positive and productive work environment. It boosts job satisfaction, improves performance, and increases retention. As a leader, empowering your team is one of the most significant investments you can make in your business's success.

## Maintaining Motivation

Motivation is the fuel that drives action. As a leader, one of your primary roles is to keep the flame of motivation burning brightly within your team. A motivated team is more productive, more innovative, and more likely to stay committed to the vision of your enterprise. Here's how you can maintain motivation:

### 1. Establish Clear Goals

Clear, achievable goals give your team a sense of purpose and direction. They provide a roadmap for what needs to be done and help team members understand how their contributions fit into the bigger picture.

### 2. Communicate the Vision

Regularly remind your team of the company's vision and its importance. Help them understand how their efforts contribute to achieving this vision. This creates a sense of belonging and purpose, which can be very motivating.

### 3. Foster a Positive Work Environment

A supportive, inclusive, and positive work environment fosters motivation. Encourage collaboration, respect diversity, and promote a culture of trust and open communication.

### 4. Recognize and Reward

Recognizing and rewarding effort and achievement is one of the most powerful motivators. Show appreciation for hard work, celebrate successes, and provide tangible rewards when possible. This not only boosts morale but also encourages continued effort.

5.  Encourage Professional Development

Offer opportunities for professional growth and skill development. This shows team members that you value them and are invested in their future. It can also help them to feel more competent and confident, increasing their motivation.

6.  Lead by Example

Be a role model of dedication, hard work, and positivity. Your enthusiasm and commitment can inspire and motivate your team.

7.  Encourage Work-Life Balance

While dedication to work is important, it's also crucial to promote a healthy work-life balance. Overwork can lead to burnout, which can drastically reduce motivation. Encourage your team to take time for rest and personal interests.

Motivation is not a one-time thing but a continuous process. As a leader, it's your responsibility to create and maintain an environment that fosters motivation. Remember, a motivated team is a successful team.

# CHAPTER 7: INNOVATIVENESS: KEEPING UP WITH CHANGE

Innovation is the heartbeat of entrepreneurship. It is the ability to generate novel and valuable ideas, and the aptitude to implement them successfully within the business framework. In today's fast-paced, ever-evolving business landscape, innovativeness is not just a competitive advantage but a necessity for survival and growth.

Innovation comes in various forms – from pioneering groundbreaking products and services, and developing new processes, to adopting cutting-edge technologies. But being innovative is not merely about creating something new; it's about continuously striving to improve and evolve, pushing boundaries, and daring to disrupt.

In this chapter, we will delve into the essence of innovativeness in entrepreneurship. We will explore how to foster a culture of innovation within your organization, how to leverage innovative thinking to stay ahead of the competition, and how to adapt to change swiftly and effectively.

Innovation is often perceived as a mysterious, elusive phenomenon. However, with the right mindset and strategies, it can be cultivated and harnessed to propel your business toward remarkable success. As you venture into this chapter, prepare to unlock the innovative entrepreneur within you and embrace the exciting world of possibilities that innovation brings.

Let's embark on this journey of discovery and transformation, as we delve into the exciting realm of entrepreneurial innovativeness. As the saying goes, "Innovation distinguishes between a leader and a follower." So, let's take the lead and inspire change, one innovative idea at a time.

## The Importance of Innovation

Innovation, in its simplest form, is about doing things differently and better. It's about breaking the status quo, daring to explore the unexplored, and finding fresh solutions to existing problems. But what makes innovation so important in the realm of entrepreneurship? Let's delve deeper:

**Driving Growth and Profitability**: Innovation opens up new avenues for growth and profitability. It can lead to the development of unique products or services, improve operational efficiency, and open up new markets. All these translate into increased revenue and profit margins.

**Creating Competitive Advantage:** In a fiercely competitive business landscape, innovation helps set your business apart. A unique, innovative offering can differentiate your brand, attract more customers, and give you an edge over your competitors.

**Addressing Customer Needs:** Innovation allows businesses to better meet the ever-evolving needs and expectations of customers. By continuously innovating, you can offer solutions that are more aligned with your customer's preferences, thereby enhancing customer satisfaction and loyalty.

**Enhancing Employee Engagement:** A culture of innovation creates an exciting and dynamic work environment. It provides employees with opportunities to express their creativity, solve problems, and make a meaningful impact, thereby boosting their engagement and productivity.

**Fostering Sustainability:** Innovation can lead to the creation of sustainable business models, products, or services that not only benefit the business but also contribute to societal and environmental well-being.

**Adapting to Change:** The business landscape is constantly changing due to shifts in market trends, customer behavior, technology, and regulations. Innovation is crucial for businesses to adapt to these changes swiftly and effectively.

The importance of innovation in entrepreneurship cannot be overstated. As Steve Jobs, co-founder of Apple Inc., rightly said, "Innovation is what separates leaders from followers." By embracing innovation, you don't just survive the competition; you lead it. Innovation is the path to continuous improvement, a unique value proposition, and ultimately entrepreneurial success.

# The Cycle of Creativity

Creativity is the genesis of innovation. It is the fountainhead of unique ideas and fresh perspectives that fuel innovative thinking. Creativity doesn't follow a linear process; instead, it moves in a cycle, a continuous loop of idea generation, evaluation, implementation, and iteration. Let's understand the different stages of the cycle of creativity:

**Inspiration:** The creative cycle begins with inspiration. It is the spark that ignites the creative process. Inspiration can strike at any moment and from anywhere – it could come from a conversation, a book, a problem you're facing, or even a random thought.

**Idea Generation:** Once inspired, your mind starts generating ideas. You explore different possibilities, brainstorm, and let your thoughts flow freely. The goal is not to find the perfect idea but to generate as many ideas as possible.

**Idea Evaluation:** Once you have a pool of ideas, the next step is to evaluate them. Here, you scrutinize each idea, weigh its pros and cons, and assess its feasibility and potential impact. The goal is to identify the ideas that are worth pursuing.

**Experimentation:** After selecting an idea, you start experimenting with it. This involves testing the idea, developing prototypes, and getting feedback. You learn by doing, making mistakes, and refining your idea based on what you learn.

**Implementation:** After refining your idea through experimentation, you move on to implement it. This involves translating your idea into action - whether it's launching a new product, introducing a new process, or implementing a new strategy.

**Review and Iteration:** After implementation, you review the outcome. You assess whether the idea achieved its intended purpose, what worked, and what didn't. Based on this evaluation, you iterate - you refine and improve your idea. This marks the completion of the creative cycle.

**Re-Inspiration:** As the cycle completes, a new one begins. The experiences and learnings from the previous cycle serve as inspiration for the new cycle.

The cycle of creativity is a continuous process of ideation, evaluation, implementation, and iteration. It's a journey of exploration, experimentation, and learning. Embrace this cycle, and let it guide your creative and innovative endeavors. Remember, as an entrepreneur, creativity is not just a tool; it's a mindset. It's about seeing possibilities where others see limitations, about challenging norms, and daring to venture into the unknown.

## Adapting to Change

Change is the only constant in the business world. Market trends shift, customer preferences evolve, technologies advance, and regulations update. In such a dynamic environment, the ability to adapt to change is not just an asset; it's a necessity for entrepreneurial survival and success. Here's how you, as an entrepreneur, can effectively adapt to change:

**Embrace Change:** The first step toward adapting to change is accepting it. Instead of resisting change, view it as an opportunity for growth and innovation. Embrace the uncertainty that comes with change and use it as a springboard to explore new possibilities.

**Stay Informed:** To adapt to change, you need to be aware of it. Stay updated on the latest trends, technologies, and industry developments. Attend seminars, read reports, follow influential figures, and be a lifelong learner.

**Foster Agility:** Agility is the capability to move quickly and easily. In business, this means being able to respond to change swiftly and effectively. Develop an agile mindset and cultivate it in your organization. Encourage flexibility, fast decision-making, and continuous learning.

**Encourage Innovation:** Innovation is a powerful tool to adapt to change. It allows you to find new ways to address emerging challenges and seize new opportunities. Foster a culture of innovation within your organization, where everyone is encouraged to think creatively and outside the box.

**Be Resilient:** Change often brings challenges. It's important to be resilient, to bounce back from setbacks, and to keep going despite obstacles. Remember, it's not the strongest species that survive, nor the most intelligent, but the ones most responsive to change.

**Involve Your Team:** Change affects everyone in the organization. Involve your team in the change process. Communicate openly about the change, its impact, and how to navigate it. Encourage feedback and collaboration.

**Plan and Prepare:** While you cannot predict every change, you can plan and prepare for it. Develop a change management strategy that outlines how to handle potential changes. This can include contingency plans, risk management strategies, and recovery plans.

Adapting to change is vital in the rapidly evolving entrepreneurial landscape. It requires openness, agility, creativity, resilience, collaboration, and foresight. As Charles Darwin said, "It is not the strongest of the species that survives, nor the most intelligent; it is the one most adaptable to change." So, gear up, embrace change, and let it propel you toward entrepreneurial success.

## Fostering a Culture of Innovation

Innovation is the lifeblood of entrepreneurship. It enables businesses to stay competitive, grow, and shape the future. However, innovation doesn't happen in a vacuum; it thrives in an environment that encourages it, that embraces it - a culture of innovation. Here's how you, as an entrepreneur, can foster a culture of innovation in your organization:

**Value Innovation:** The first step toward fostering a culture of innovation is to value it. Innovation should be a part of your organization's vision, mission, and values. It should be seen as a strategic priority, not as an optional extra.

**Lead by Example:** As a leader, your actions set the tone for the organization. Show your commitment to innovation through your actions. Encourage innovative thinking, take calculated risks, and embrace learning and change.

**Create a Safe Space:** Innovation involves trying new things and taking risks, which can lead to failures. Create an environment where failures are seen as opportunities for learning, not as reasons for punishment. Make your organization a safe space for taking risks and making mistakes.

**Encourage Diverse Thinking:** Innovation thrives on diversity of thought. Encourage diverse thinking by creating a diverse team and by fostering an inclusive environment where all voices are heard and respected.

**Provide Resources:** Innovation needs resources – time, tools, and training. Allocate dedicated time for innovation, provide tools that aid creative thinking, and offer training in creative problem-solving techniques.

**Facilitate Collaboration:** Innovation often emerges from the intersection of different ideas, disciplines, and experiences.

Facilitate collaboration within and across teams, departments, and even organizations. Foster a culture where everyone is encouraged to share ideas and insights.

**Recognize and Reward Innovation:** People are more likely to engage in innovative behaviors when they are recognized and rewarded. Set up systems to recognize and reward innovative efforts, even when they don't lead to successful outcomes.

**Iterate and Evolve:** Innovation is a continuous process. It's about constantly seeking ways to improve and evolve. Encourage an iterative mindset, where ideas are continually refined, tested, and improved.

Fostering a culture of innovation is not a one-time task. It's a continuous endeavor that requires commitment, leadership, and effort. But the rewards are worth it. A culture of innovation not only fuels business growth and success but also makes the entrepreneurial journey more exciting and fulfilling. So, embrace innovation, make it a part of your organizational culture, and watch how it propels your business toward new horizons.

# CHAPTER 8: RISK-TAKING: THE ENTREPRENEUR'S GAMBLE

Venturing into the world of entrepreneurship is like stepping into a game of high-stakes poker. The risks are great, the uncertainties many, and the outcomes unpredictable. Yet, it is these very elements of risk and uncertainty that often hold the key to remarkable success and innovation. Risk-taking is inherent to entrepreneurship. The decision to launch a new venture, to invest in an unproven idea, to venture into unknown markets - each of these is a gamble, a risk taken in the pursuit of entrepreneurial success.

In this chapter titled "Risk-Taking: The Entrepreneur's Gamble," we will explore the pivotal role of risk-taking in entrepreneurship. We will dive deep into understanding the nature of risk, why it's an integral part of entrepreneurship, and how successful entrepreneurs manage and harness risk to their advantage.

Through detailed discussions and real-life examples, we aim to equip you with the knowledge and skills necessary to handle risks effectively. We will delve into topics such as understanding and assessing risks, the balance between risk and reward, how to mitigate and manage risks, and the art of taking calculated risks.

Entrepreneurship is not for the faint-hearted, and this chapter is not about eliminating risks - that's an impossible task. Instead, it's about learning to dance with uncertainties, turning the odds in your favor, and making the most of the entrepreneurial gamble.

So, are you ready to take the plunge, roll the dice, and navigate the exhilarating journey of entrepreneurial risk-taking? Let's dive in!

## Decoding Risk

Risk. The word itself evokes a sense of unease, potential danger, and uncertainty. However, in the realm of entrepreneurship, risk carries a different connotation. It becomes an essential element of the journey, a challenge to overcome, a dance to be learned. Let's decode the concept of risk and understand its intrinsic relationship with entrepreneurship.

Risk is the possibility of an adverse event occurring that can lead to losses or damages. In entrepreneurship, risk can manifest in various forms - financial risk, market risk, operational risk, or strategic risk, among others. These risks may arise due to factors such as market volatility, competitive dynamics, technological changes, or management decisions.

Entrepreneurship is inherently risky due to the uncertainties involved. Entrepreneurs venture into uncharted territories, launching new products or services, targeting unexplored markets, or employing untested strategies. They often stake their personal finances, time, and reputation on the success of their venture. The possibility of failure and the associated losses is real and significant.

However, viewing risk only as a potential hazard is a narrow perspective. Risk also embodies opportunities. The entrepreneur's gamble lies in exploiting these opportunities, and in leveraging risks to their advantage. Successful entrepreneurs are not reckless risk-takers; instead, they are calculated risk-takers. They understand that risk and reward are two sides of the same coin - the greater the risk, the higher the potential reward. They perceive risk as a necessary stepping stone toward their entrepreneurial goals.

Decoding risk involves understanding its dual nature - its potential for both loss and gain. It requires recognizing the various sources of risk and being aware of the potential impact of these risks on the venture. More importantly, it involves developing the mindset to view risk not as a barrier but as a catalyst for innovation, growth, and success.

In this entrepreneurship journey, risk will be your constant companion. The key is not to avoid risks but to understand them, manage them, and turn them into opportunities. As we venture further into this chapter, we will explore how you can master the art of risk-taking and use it to fuel your entrepreneurial success.

## Evaluating Pros and Cons

Taking risks is part and parcel of entrepreneurship, but it doesn't imply jumping headfirst into any and every opportunity that comes your way. It's about taking calculated risks. The foundation of calculated risk-taking lies in evaluating the pros and cons - assessing the potential benefits and drawbacks before making a decision.

Evaluation starts with understanding the nature of the risk involved. What kind of risk are you dealing with? Is it a financial risk, such as the potential loss of capital? Or is it a strategic risk, like entering a new market or launching a new product? Maybe it's an operational risk, linked to the daily operations of your business, or a compliance risk, associated with regulatory requirements. Identifying the type of risk gives clarity about its potential impact.

Once the risk is understood, the next step is to weigh its pros and cons. This involves estimating the potential benefits and drawbacks associated with the risk. Consider the best-case scenario, the worst-case scenario, and the most likely outcome. Try to quantify the impact in terms of finances, time, resources, reputation, and other relevant factors. Use data, research, and analysis to make this estimation as objective as possible.

Evaluating pros and cons isn't only about numbers, it also involves considering the qualitative aspects. For instance, how does the risk align with your business goals and values? How would it impact your stakeholders - employees, customers, investors, etc.? Does it align with your risk tolerance level and your long-term strategic plans?

Additionally, consider the opportunity cost - what would be the cost of not taking the risk? In the dynamic world of entrepreneurship, not taking a risk can be as consequential as taking one. Missing out on opportunities might lead to stagnation and inhibit growth.

Evaluating pros and cons is a critical step in risk management. It enables you to make informed decisions, reduces uncertainty, and helps in developing contingency plans. It allows you to take calculated risks, where the potential benefits outweigh the potential drawbacks.

As we move further into this chapter, we will discuss how to leverage this evaluation to formulate effective risk management strategies. The goal is to equip you with the knowledge and skills to navigate the risk landscape confidently and turn risks into opportunities for growth and success.

## Courage to Leap

Every entrepreneurial journey requires a leap of faith. You can conduct extensive research, draft detailed business plans, and prepare for contingencies, but at some point, you have to gather your courage and jump. You have to take the risk and leap into the unknown. This chapter, "Courage to Leap," explores that critical moment when an entrepreneur decides to embrace risk, trust their instincts, and step into the world of uncertainties.

It is important to understand that the leap of faith is not about being reckless or hasty. Instead, it's about having the courage to act despite the uncertainties, about believing in your abilities to navigate the challenges and to make the most of the opportunities that come your way.

What fuels this courage? The answer lies in your preparation and mindset. When you have conducted a thorough evaluation of the risks and rewards, when you have a well-thought-out strategy, and when you are mentally prepared to handle failures and setbacks, you are better equipped to leap. You have the confidence to take the risk because you understand it, you are prepared for it, and you are ready to leverage it.

Furthermore, the courage to leap stems from your passion and commitment to your entrepreneurial goals. It comes from your belief in your idea and your vision. It is fueled by your determination to create a positive impact, bring change, and make a difference through your entrepreneurial venture.

That said, the leap of faith is not a one-time event. Throughout your entrepreneurial journey, you will encounter numerous instances where you will need to take risks, make tough decisions, and step out of your comfort zone. The courage to leap is not just about launching the venture; it's about continuously navigating the uncertain and challenging landscape of entrepreneurship.

So, how do you foster this courage? How do you prepare yourself to leap, again and again, throughout your entrepreneurial journey? The upcoming sections will provide insights into building resilience, developing a risk-taking mindset, and cultivating the courage to leap. The goal is to empower you with the confidence and courage to embrace risk, navigate uncertainties, and pave the path toward your entrepreneurial success.

## *Managing and Mitigating Risks*

Risk-taking forms the backbone of entrepreneurship, but success lies in your ability to manage and mitigate these risks effectively. This chapter, "Managing and Mitigating Risks," aims to arm you with the knowledge and tools to not only confront risks head-on but also to reduce their potential impact and turn them into opportunities.

Risk management begins with risk identification. By recognizing the potential risks that you could face, you can begin to develop strategies to counteract them. These risks can be internal or external, and span from financial and operational risks to strategic and compliance risks. Rigorous risk identification provides a holistic view of the challenges that could arise and the impacts they could have on your venture.

Following risk identification comes risk assessment. This involves evaluating the likelihood of a risk materializing and its potential impact on your business. It's about determining which risks are most significant and requires immediate attention and which risks can be accepted and monitored. A risk matrix, a tool that maps out the severity and likelihood of risks, can be useful in prioritizing risks.

Once the risks have been identified and assessed, you can start developing risk response strategies. These strategies depend on the nature of the risk and your risk tolerance level. They generally fall into four categories: avoidance (eliminating the risk), reduction (minimizing the impact of the risk), transfer (shifting the risk to another party), and acceptance (acknowledging the risk and preparing to deal with its consequences).

Implementing these strategies involves developing action plans, assigning responsibilities, setting timelines, and allocating resources. It's about preparing your team to respond swiftly and effectively when a risk materializes. A key component of risk response is contingency planning - having a Plan B in case the risk materializes and impacts your business.

Risk management is an ongoing process. It requires continuous monitoring and reviewing. As your business grows and evolves, and as the external environment changes, new risks may emerge, and existing risks may change. Regularly reviewing your risk management plans and updating them as necessary ensures they remain relevant and effective.

Remember, the goal of risk management is not to eliminate all risks. That would be not only impossible but also undesirable, as taking risks is integral to innovation and growth. The aim is to manage risks in a way that you can still take bold steps forward without jeopardizing your entrepreneurial venture. As we delve deeper into this topic, we will equip you with practical tools and techniques to manage and mitigate risks effectively, enabling you to transform uncertainties into opportunities for growth and success.

# CHAPTER 9: EMOTIONAL INTELLIGENCE: THE UNSPOKEN POWER

While our society often lauds and values intellect, there is another form of intelligence that frequently goes unrecognized and underappreciated. This form of intelligence, emotional intelligence, or EQ is as crucial, if not more, to a successful entrepreneurial journey as the traditional intelligence quotient, or IQ. This chapter, "Emotional Intelligence: The Unspoken Power," seeks to shed light on the pivotal role of emotional intelligence in entrepreneurship.

As an entrepreneur, you do not operate in a vacuum. You interact with a variety of stakeholders - from your employees and customers to your investors and suppliers. How well you understand, manage, and leverage these relationships significantly impacts your venture's success. And at the core of these interactions lies emotional intelligence.

Emotional intelligence is about being aware of and understanding your emotions and those of others. It's about managing your emotions in a way that contributes positively to your objectives. It's about using your emotional awareness to guide your decision-making and to improve your relationships. In short, emotional intelligence is about using your emotions intelligently.

Emotional intelligence in entrepreneurship manifests in various ways. It can be seen in an entrepreneur's empathy when dealing with their employees, in their emotional stability when navigating turbulent times, or in their interpersonal skills when networking with potential investors. It can also be seen in their self-awareness, which aids them in assessing their strengths and weaknesses, and in their self-regulation, which helps them to keep their impulses in check.

Throughout this chapter, we will delve deeper into the concept of emotional intelligence, exploring its five key components: self-awareness, self-regulation, motivation, empathy, and social skills. We will look at how these elements impact various aspects of your entrepreneurial journey, from decision-making and leadership to resilience and stress management. Furthermore, we will offer insights and practical strategies to enhance your emotional intelligence, empowering you to leverage this unspoken power for your entrepreneurial success.

Prepare to dive into an exploration of the emotional realm of entrepreneurship, a realm that, while often overlooked, holds the key to effective leadership, strong relationships, and sustainable success. Let's embark on this journey to unlock the power of emotional intelligence.

To fully unlock the power of emotional intelligence, we must first seek to understand its nature and scope. So, what exactly is emotional intelligence?

In its simplest form, emotional intelligence is the capacity to understand and manage your own emotions and those of the people around you. Introduced by psychologists Peter Salovey and John Mayer in the 1990s and popularized by psychologist and science journalist Daniel Goleman, emotional intelligence has become increasingly recognized as a critical factor in personal and professional success.

Emotional intelligence, often abbreviated as EI or EQ (emotional quotient), is composed of four core components: self-awareness, self-management, social awareness, and relationship management.

1. **Self-awareness**: This is the ability to recognize and understand your own emotions and their effects on your behavior and thoughts. It involves knowing your strengths and limitations and having a clear perception of your self-image. Self-aware individuals are more likely to understand how their feelings affect them, the people around them, and their job performance.

2. **Self-management**: This is the ability to manage your emotional reactions to all situations and people. Self-management involves being able to stay in control and calm under pressure while remaining flexible and adaptable to changing circumstances.

3. **Social awareness**: This aspect of EQ refers to the ability to understand the emotions and needs of others. It involves empathy, organizational awareness, and recognizing and appreciating the dynamics of

relationships.

4. **Relationship management**: This involves being able to develop and maintain good relationships, communicate clearly, inspire and influence others, work well in a team, and manage conflict.

Contrary to popular belief, emotional intelligence is not the opposite of intelligence, the triumph of heart over head—it is the unique intersection of both. It enables individuals to channel their emotions to deal with life's challenges, build positive social interactions, make personal decisions that achieve positive results, and cope with emotional demands maturely and respectfully.

For entrepreneurs, EQ is a valuable tool. It aids in effective decision-making, building and leading teams, handling stress, overcoming challenges, and creating strong business relationships. Having high emotional intelligence can lead to better outcomes in negotiations, leadership effectiveness, job performance, and mental health.

As we journey through this chapter, we will dissect each of these four components, shedding light on their influence in entrepreneurial settings and providing practical advice on how to strengthen each of these emotional intelligence skills. Let's embark on this enlightening journey of emotional self-discovery and growth.

## Mastering Self-Awareness

Self-awareness is the foundation of emotional intelligence. It involves knowing your feelings and emotions, understanding what triggers them, and recognizing how they affect your thoughts and behaviors. Self-awareness also includes the ability to identify your strengths and weaknesses objectively, maintain a well-grounded sense of self-confidence, and understand how others perceive you.

For an entrepreneur, self-awareness is not just about knowing who you are, but also about understanding your impact on others. This awareness allows you to adjust your behaviors and reactions to achieve the best results in different situations.

So, how can you increase your self-awareness?

1. **Mindfulness and Reflection**: Mindfulness involves focusing on the present moment without judgment. It enables you to become aware of your current emotions and understand them better. Complement this with regular reflection, where you take time to introspect your thoughts, feelings, and reactions. Reflecting on both successes and failures can offer valuable insights into your emotional patterns and reactions.

2. **Seek Feedback**: Feedback from others can provide a different perspective and help you understand how your actions and emotions are perceived by others. This can be from trusted colleagues, mentors, or friends. Be open to feedback and be willing to accept it as a tool for growth, not criticism.

3. **Keep a Journal**: Documenting your thoughts, feelings, and experiences in a journal can help you track your emotional patterns over time. This can help you identify emotional triggers and how you typically react to certain situations.

4. **Practice Self-Questioning**: Regularly question your emotions. Why am I feeling this way? What caused this emotion? How am I reacting to it? How is it affecting my decision-making or relationships? This line of questioning can help you understand your emotions and reactions better.

5. **Develop Emotional Vocabulary**: Being able to accurately label your feelings is a critical part of self-awareness. It allows you to recognize, communicate, and manage your emotions more effectively.

Mastering self-awareness is not an overnight task. It's an ongoing process that requires time, commitment, and a lot of introspection. But it's a journey worth embarking on. A high level of self-awareness enables you to navigate your entrepreneurial journey with more wisdom, control, and adaptability. Remember, you cannot manage what you are not aware of. Your journey to effective emotional intelligence starts with mastering self-awareness.

# Managing Emotions: Yours and Others

Once we are aware of our emotions and the emotions of those around us, the next step in emotional intelligence is to manage these emotions effectively. Managing emotions involves regulating our feelings, responding appropriately to the emotions of others, and using emotions to facilitate thinking and guide decision-making.

For an entrepreneur, emotional management is crucial. It can mean the difference between a well-handled crisis and a catastrophe, between a motivated team and a dispirited one, and between success and failure in the business world.

Here's how you can improve your emotional management:

1. **Emotional Self-Control**: This involves keeping disruptive emotions and impulses in check. It's not about suppressing or ignoring your emotions, but rather acknowledging them and choosing an appropriate response. Techniques such as deep breathing, meditation, and mindfulness can help you develop better emotional self-control.

2. **Use Emotions to Facilitate Thinking**: Positive emotions can enhance problem-solving skills and promote creative thinking. When faced with a challenge, instead of succumbing to stress or fear, channel your emotions toward finding a solution. Embrace positive emotions like curiosity and excitement to fuel your creativity and drive your decision-making.

3. **Understand Others' Emotions**: As an entrepreneur, you're often in a leadership role. Understanding your team's emotions can help you respond appropriately

and manage team dynamics effectively. Empathy is key here – it allows you to sense and understand the feelings of others, helping you communicate effectively and build stronger relationships.

4. **Handle Relationships Well**: Managing relationships involves influencing others, managing conflict, inspiring and guiding others, and working well in a team. Developing these skills can help you build a motivated team, resolve disputes effectively, and create a positive working environment.

5. **Practice Responding, Not Reacting**: There's a crucial difference between reacting and responding. Reactions are often emotional and not thought through, while responses are calculated and involve consideration of the situation and possible outcomes. By practicing mindful responses, you can manage situations more effectively.

Remember, managing emotions doesn't mean becoming emotionless. Emotions are a natural part of human behavior and provide valuable information about our reactions to experiences. The goal is to understand and manage these emotions, using them as a tool to guide thinking and behavior, rather than letting them control us.

In the entrepreneurial journey, emotional management can help you maintain balance during the highs and lows, make thoughtful decisions, build stronger business relationships, and lead your team effectively. Developing these skills can set you apart in the business world and contribute significantly to your success as an entrepreneur.

## Enhancing Interpersonal Skills

Interpersonal skills, often referred to as people skills or social skills, are the abilities we use to interact and communicate with others. They include a wide range of skills, but some of the most important are active listening, empathy, patience, communication, and the ability to understand and respect the perspectives of others.

For an entrepreneur, strong interpersonal skills are essential. They help in building and maintaining strong relationships with employees, partners, customers, and investors. They can also help in conflict resolution, team building, and problem-solving.

Here are some strategies for enhancing your interpersonal skills:

1. **Active Listening**: This is more than just hearing what someone else is saying. Active listening involves fully concentrating, understanding, responding, and then remembering what is being said. It shows the speaker that you value their thoughts and are engaged in the conversation.

2. **Effective Communication**: Clear, concise communication is key to avoiding misunderstandings and building trust. This includes both verbal and non-verbal communication. Be aware of your body language and tone of voice, as these can also convey messages to the listener.

3. **Empathy**: This involves understanding and sharing the feelings of others. When you empathize with others, you can better understand their needs and perspectives, which can lead to more meaningful, respectful interactions.

4. **Patience**: Not everyone thinks or communicates in the same way you do. Patience allows for better understanding and helps prevent unnecessary conflict.

5. **Conflict Resolution**: Disagreements are inevitable when working with others. The ability to find solutions to conflicts in a fair, unbiased way is a valuable interpersonal skill.

6. **Respect for Others**: This involves recognizing and appreciating the value, diversity, and contribution of others. Respectful interaction encourages open communication, mutual trust, and collaborative relationships.

7. **Assertiveness**: This is the ability to express your thoughts, beliefs, and desires in a direct, honest, and appropriate way. It is not about being aggressive, but rather about standing up for your rights while respecting the rights of others.

As an entrepreneur, enhancing your interpersonal skills can lead to more productive relationships, a more harmonious work environment, and better business outcomes. Remember, businesses are built on relationships, and strong interpersonal skills are the foundation of successful relationships.

# CHAPTER 10: PERSISTENCE: THE ROAD LESS TRAVELED

Persistence, often regarded as one of the most commendable qualities an entrepreneur can possess, is the gritty determination that propels individuals to continue moving forward, no matter the size of the hurdles that stand in their way. It's the audacious insistence on reaching your goals, irrespective of the challenges and setbacks that you might encounter.

When faced with failure, uncertainty, or hardship, it's persistence that drives one to rise, dust off, and venture forth once again. It's about learning from your mistakes, refining your approach, and relentlessly pursuing your ambitions. Persistence is not simply about never giving up; it's about continually improving and relentlessly pursuing your goals, regardless of how many times you may stumble.

In the entrepreneurial realm, the path is rarely linear. There are countless stories of companies that faced almost insurmountable difficulties, only to eventually attain monumental success. What unites these narratives is the entrepreneur's relentless persistence.

In this chapter, we will explore the concept of persistence in-depth, seeking to understand its importance, how it can be cultivated, and how it can be applied effectively in the world of entrepreneurship. This journey will take us through the winding paths of maintaining unwavering focus, dealing with rejection, handling criticism, and staying motivated during difficult times.

Just as the mighty river eventually carves its way through the mountain, not by power, but by persistent movement, we, too, can shape our entrepreneurial journey through the power of persistence. So, let's delve deeper into this intriguing journey of unwavering resolve, and persistence – the road less traveled.

## Defining Persistence

The dictionary defines persistence as a firm or obstinate continuance in a course of action despite difficulty or opposition. In the context of entrepreneurship, it takes on a deeper meaning. It is the unyielding spirit that refuses to give up, a quality that allows entrepreneurs to keep pushing forward in the face of adversity, and to persevere through the various challenges that stand in the way of their goals.

Persistence, however, is more than just stubbornly clinging to an idea or a plan. It also involves the ability to be adaptable and flexible, to learn from failures and mistakes, and to continually seek ways to improve and refine one's approach. It's about having the strength to face rejection and criticism, the resilience to bounce back from setbacks, and the courage to take risks, even in the face of uncertainty.

For an entrepreneur, persistence is the ability to keep the end goal in sight, while navigating through the twists and turns of the journey. It's about seeing past the immediate hurdles and maintaining the belief that with enough effort and determination, success is achievable. It's an amalgamation of resilience, determination, patience, and adaptability.

Persistence is often what separates successful entrepreneurs from those who fail. It is easy to give up when things get tough or when a venture does not go as planned. But those who persist, who pick themselves up and try again and again, are the ones who ultimately achieve their goals.

So, in essence, persistence is the unwavering commitment to success, the refusal to be deterred by failure, the tenacity to keep going in the face of adversity, and the adaptability to learn and grow from every experience. It's the indefatigable spirit that defines the true essence of an entrepreneur.

# Building Stamina for
## Long-term Goals

The road to entrepreneurial success is often long and arduous. It requires patience, discipline, and the ability to maintain focus on long-term goals despite the inevitable obstacles and setbacks. This is where stamina comes in. Stamina, much like persistence, is about enduring hardship, but it's specifically about the ability to exert oneself for prolonged periods. It's the fuel that allows entrepreneurs to keep moving toward their goals, even when the road gets tough.

Building stamina for long-term goals is a multi-faceted process. It starts with developing a strong, clear vision of what you want to achieve. This vision acts as your North Star, guiding you through the inevitable ups and downs of the entrepreneurial journey. The more vivid and tangible your long-term goals are, the easier it will be to stay focused and committed.

Next, stamina is cultivated through consistent action. It's not about sprinting toward your goal; it's about moving steadily, maintaining a pace that you can sustain over the long run. It's about understanding that success is a marathon, not a sprint and that every step, no matter how small, is bringing you closer to your destination.

Self-care also plays a vital role in building stamina. This includes maintaining a healthy lifestyle, ensuring adequate sleep, managing stress effectively, and taking time to recharge and rejuvenate. Without taking care of your physical, mental, and emotional well-being, it's easy to burn out, making it much harder to stay persistent.

Finally, building stamina requires a growth mindset. This means embracing challenges as opportunities for learning and growth, rather than viewing them as insurmountable obstacles.

It's about understanding that the path to success is paved with failures, mistakes, and setbacks and that each of these is a stepping stone on the journey toward your goals.

Building stamina for long-term goals is about endurance and consistency, taking care of your well-being, and maintaining a positive, growth-oriented mindset. With these strategies, you can cultivate the stamina necessary to persist on the often challenging road of entrepreneurship, propelling you ever closer to your entrepreneurial dreams.

## Overcoming Obstacles

Every entrepreneurial journey is characterized by a variety of obstacles. These obstacles may be internal, such as fear of failure, lack of self-confidence, or inability to make tough decisions. Or they may be external, such as market competition, financial constraints, or lack of consumer interest. However, a key attribute of successful entrepreneurs is their ability to overcome these obstacles, transforming them into opportunities for growth and improvement.

The first step to overcoming obstacles is acknowledging their existence. Entrepreneurs often need to develop a sense of self-awareness, identifying their weaknesses and the external threats that could derail their efforts. This can be achieved through reflective practices, feedback from others, or even formal assessment tools.

Once obstacles have been identified, they must be faced head-on. This involves creating a plan of action to address each obstacle. This plan may involve acquiring new skills, seeking advice from mentors, diversifying business practices, or securing additional funding. These plans must be flexible, as what works in one situation may not be effective in another.

An essential tool in overcoming obstacles is a positive mindset. Rather than viewing obstacles as insurmountable roadblocks, successful entrepreneurs see them as challenges to be conquered. This mindset shift can drastically alter an entrepreneur's approach to problem-solving, promoting creativity, innovation, and resilience.

Finally, overcoming obstacles requires persistence and resilience. Setbacks and failures are often not only probable but inevitable in any entrepreneurial journey. The ability to bounce back from these setbacks, learn from mistakes and move forward with renewed determination, is what sets successful entrepreneurs apart.

In conclusion, overcoming obstacles is an integral part of the entrepreneurial journey. Through self-awareness, strategic planning, a positive mindset, and relentless persistence, entrepreneurs can turn obstacles into stepping stones on their path to success.

# Cultivating Discipline and Determination

Discipline and determination are two core characteristics that underpin entrepreneurial success. They are the invisible forces that propel entrepreneurs forward, guiding them to persist in the face of adversity and to stay committed to their long-term goals. Cultivating these traits is a critical step on the entrepreneurial journey.

Discipline is the ability to stay focused and committed to your goals despite distractions or difficulties. It involves setting a clear path and adhering to it, regardless of the challenges that arise. This requires planning and organizing your tasks, managing your time effectively, and maintaining a strong work ethic. It's about doing what needs to be done, even when you don't feel like it.

Determination, on the other hand, is the unwavering resolve to achieve your goals, no matter the odds. It's the grit and resilience that keeps you moving forward when faced with setbacks or failures. It's the refusal to give up, no matter how challenging the journey may become.

Cultivating discipline starts with setting clear, measurable goals. These goals act as a roadmap, guiding your actions and helping you stay focused. Once your goals are set, create a detailed plan outlining the steps you'll take to achieve them. This plan should be reviewed and adjusted regularly to reflect your progress and any changes in your circumstances.

To build determination, begin by adopting a growth mindset. View challenges as opportunities for learning and growth, rather than obstacles. Celebrate your successes, no matter how small, and use your failures as lessons to improve and evolve.

Surrounding yourself with positive, like-minded individuals can also bolster your determination, as their support and encouragement can help you stay motivated during tough times.

Finally, remember that discipline and determination are like muscles – they grow stronger with practice. Start small, setting manageable goals and gradually pushing yourself to achieve more. Over time, your discipline and determination will grow, fueling your journey toward entrepreneurial success.

In conclusion, cultivating discipline and determination is a crucial part of the entrepreneurial journey. These traits will guide you as you navigate the challenges and uncertainties of entrepreneurship, keeping you focused, motivated, and committed to achieving your entrepreneurial dreams.

# CHAPTER 11:
# DECISION-MAKING:
# THE POWER OF
# CHOICES

Decision-making is an art. It's an integral part of our everyday lives, from mundane choices like what to have for breakfast to life-altering decisions like starting a new venture. In the world of entrepreneurship, decision-making acquires a heightened significance. Each choice an entrepreneur makes can set the trajectory for their business's growth, success, or failure.

The eleventh chapter of our entrepreneurial journey, "Decision-Making: The Power of Choices," delves deep into the heart of this critical aspect of entrepreneurship. It uncovers the dynamics of effective decision-making and elucidates how entrepreneurs can harness the power of their choices to steer their ventures toward success.

In this chapter, we will unravel the intricate process of decision-making, starting with understanding what decision-making truly means in an entrepreneurial context. We will shed light on the steps involved in making an informed decision and the pitfalls to avoid. We will also introduce various decision-making models and tools that entrepreneurs can utilize to make optimal choices.

Entrepreneurship often demands quick, yet well-thought-out

decisions. Therefore, we will discuss the balance between speed and accuracy in decision-making and explore how entrepreneurs can maintain this balance under different circumstances. We will also delve into the crucial role of intuition in entrepreneurial decision-making, examining its interplay with data-driven decisions.

Lastly, this chapter will illuminate the power of reflective decision-making. We will explore how entrepreneurs can learn from their past choices, both successful and unsuccessful ones, to make better decisions in the future.

So, prepare to step into the shoes of an entrepreneur and understand the power that lies within each decision they make. As you navigate through this chapter, you will not only develop an appreciation for the complexity and significance of entrepreneurial decision-making but also equip yourself with practical tools and strategies to make effective decisions in your entrepreneurial journey.

## The Role of Decision-Making

Decisions are the lifeblood of entrepreneurship. Every day, entrepreneurs are faced with numerous decisions, both big and small, that shape the course of their businesses. From choosing the right business model to selecting the ideal team members, from defining the product roadmap to crafting the marketing strategy—every facet of entrepreneurship is infused with decisions. The role of decision-making in entrepreneurship, therefore, is paramount.

In its simplest form, decision-making can be described as the process of making choices among different alternatives. But for an entrepreneur, it's much more than that. It's about steering the ship of their venture amidst the tumultuous sea of uncertainties. It's about taking calculated risks that can yield high rewards. It's about shaping the future of their dream with their own hands.

The role of decision-making in entrepreneurship is multi-faceted and can be broken down into several key areas:

1. **Strategy Formulation:** Decisions play a critical role in forming the strategy of a business. Entrepreneurs have to make decisions about their target market, competitive positioning, growth strategy, and more. These choices directly impact the direction in which the business grows and evolves.

2. **Risk Management:** Entrepreneurship involves inherent risks. Decisions related to risk assessment, risk tolerance, and risk management are critical. Entrepreneurs need to decide when to take risks, when to avoid them, and how to mitigate them effectively.

3. **Resource Allocation:** Every business operates with finite resources. Entrepreneurs must make decisions about how to allocate these resources—money, time,

personnel, etc.—to achieve maximum efficiency and productivity.

4. **Problem-Solving:** Problems and challenges are constant in business. Decision-making is vital in choosing the best solutions to overcome these challenges.

5. **Innovation and Change:** Decision-making drives innovation. Entrepreneurs have to make choices about adopting new technologies, entering new markets, creating new products, or changing business processes.

In essence, decision-making is the engine that propels a business forward. It is the process through which entrepreneurs translate their vision into reality. It is the mechanism through which they navigate the complexities of the business world, steer clear of potential pitfalls, and guide their venture toward success. Understanding the critical role of decision-making is the first step toward mastering this essential entrepreneurial skill.

## Analyzing Situations

Analyzing situations is a crucial step in the decision-making process. It involves a thorough examination of the context or environment in which a decision has to be made. This analysis enables entrepreneurs to grasp the complexities of a situation, discern the elements at play, and understand the potential implications of their decisions.

1. **Understanding the Context:** The first step in analyzing a situation is to understand its context. This includes understanding the current state of the business, market dynamics, competition, customer preferences, and any other factors that could impact the decision. The entrepreneur needs to be cognizant of the wider business environment and how it may influence the outcome of their decision.

2. **Identifying Key Variables:** Once the context is understood, the next step is to identify the key variables in the situation. These are the elements that are likely to influence the decision or be influenced by it. For instance, in a decision about introducing a new product, key variables could include customer demand, product development costs, competition, market trends, and more.

3. **Gathering Information:** Analyzing a situation requires ample information. Entrepreneurs need to gather as much relevant data as possible about the key variables. This could involve market research, customer surveys, competitive analysis, financial modeling, and more. The quality of the decision often hinges on the quality of the information upon which it is based.

4. **Evaluating the Impact:** Every decision has

consequences. Entrepreneurs need to evaluate the potential impact of their decision. This could include direct effects, such as changes in revenue or profitability, as well as indirect effects, like changes in customer satisfaction, brand reputation, or employee morale.

5. **Anticipating Challenges:** Finally, analyzing a situation involves anticipating the challenges that might arise from a decision. This allows entrepreneurs to plan for these challenges and devise strategies to overcome them.

In essence, analyzing situations equips entrepreneurs with the knowledge and insights necessary to make informed decisions. It helps them understand the landscape in which they are operating, recognize the forces at play, and foresee the potential outcomes of their decisions. By mastering this crucial step in the decision-making process, entrepreneurs can significantly increase their chances of making successful decisions.

## Making Informed Choices

Making informed choices is the crux of decision-making. After analyzing the situation, it's time to weigh the pros and cons of different alternatives and make a choice. However, making informed choices is not merely about selecting an option that appears most beneficial on the surface. It's about making a well-thought-out decision that aligns with your business goals and values.

1. **Weighing the Options:** Having analyzed the situation and understood the potential implications, entrepreneurs should evaluate each option on its merits. This involves weighing the potential benefits against the associated risks and costs. It requires understanding not only the immediate effects but also the long-term consequences.

2. **Aligning with Objectives:** Each choice should align with the entrepreneur's broader business objectives and values. Making decisions that contradict the business's vision or mission can lead to unwanted results and negative consequences.

3. **Seeking Input:** While entrepreneurs are the primary decision-makers, they need not make decisions in isolation. Seeking input from team members, mentors, or experts can offer valuable perspectives and insights. Diverse viewpoints can help identify potential pitfalls and blind spots, leading to more informed and balanced choices.

4. **Making the Decision:** Once all alternatives have been thoroughly evaluated, it's time to make the decision. This step requires conviction and courage. Entrepreneurs need to trust their analysis and judgment, make the choice, and stand by it.

5. **Reviewing and Learning:** After a decision is made and implemented, it's crucial to review its outcomes. Did it yield the expected results? Were there unforeseen consequences? What can be learned for future decisions? This reflective process helps entrepreneurs refine their decision-making skills over time.

Making informed choices is a delicate balancing act. It requires careful analysis, strategic thinking, intuition, and courage. By following these steps, entrepreneurs can make decisions that drive their business forward, navigate challenges, and pave the way for sustained success.

## Dealing with Consequences

Every decision, big or small, comes with its consequences. While entrepreneurs strive to make the best decisions based on their available information and analysis, the outcomes may not always align with expectations. Dealing with consequences — whether positive or negative — is a vital aspect of the entrepreneurial journey.

1. **Embracing Positive Outcomes:** When a decision leads to positive results, it's a cause for celebration. It reinforces confidence in one's judgment and decision-making capabilities. Positive outcomes should be embraced, analyzed for the factors leading to success, and lessons drawn should be applied to future decisions.

2. **Learning from Negative Outcomes:** Not all decisions lead to success. Sometimes, even the most informed choices can have negative consequences due to unforeseen factors or shifts in the business environment. Rather than feeling discouraged, entrepreneurs should treat these instances as learning opportunities. It's essential to assess what went wrong, understand the factors that led to the adverse outcome, and learn how to avoid similar missteps in the future.

3. **Managing Unintended Consequences:** Sometimes, decisions may have unintended or indirect consequences. These could be impacts on staff morale, customer satisfaction, or the business's reputation. Entrepreneurs need to be aware of these potential side effects and have contingency plans in place to manage them.

4. **Adjusting the Course:** In light of the consequences

of a decision, entrepreneurs may need to adjust their course. This could mean revising strategies, rethinking objectives, or even revising the decision if the consequences prove too harmful. Flexibility and adaptability are key traits of successful entrepreneurs.

5. **Building Resilience:** Dealing with the consequences of decisions, particularly negative ones, requires resilience. It's important to bounce back from setbacks, maintain optimism, and continue moving forward. Resilience, in the face of consequences, is what sets successful entrepreneurs apart.

Dealing with consequences is a part and parcel of the entrepreneurial journey. It offers valuable lessons and insights that refine an entrepreneur's decision-making skills and shape their path to success. It is through this continuous process of decision-making, facing the consequences, and learning that entrepreneurs build their businesses, overcome challenges, and achieve their goals.

# CHAPTER 12:
# FINANCIAL ACUMEN: MASTERING THE LANGUAGE OF BUSINESS

In business, numbers tell the story. They reveal a company's health, its growth, the fruits of its labor, and areas requiring improvement. Financial acumen is an essential skill that every entrepreneur needs to master to navigate the complex and dynamic world of business successfully. Yet, many aspiring entrepreneurs, especially those with non-financial backgrounds, often feel intimidated by financial jargon and the seeming complexity of financial statements.

Chapter Twelve, "Financial Acumen: Mastering the Language of Business," is dedicated to unraveling the mystery surrounding business finance. It aims to simplify the concepts and equip entrepreneurs with the necessary skills to understand and use financial information effectively.

In this chapter, we will dive deep into the importance of financial literacy for entrepreneurs. We will decode key financial statements and their components and discuss budgeting and financial planning for a business's growth. We will also touch upon investment principles and capital management, which are critical for scaling businesses.

Developing a strong financial acumen not only enables entrepreneurs to make informed business decisions but also equips them to communicate effectively with stakeholders, negotiate better with vendors and lenders, and attract potential investors.

By the end of this chapter, readers should have a firm grasp on the basics of business finance and feel empowered to use this knowledge for the benefit of their entrepreneurial endeavors. Whether you're just starting your entrepreneurial journey or looking to grow and expand your business, mastering the language of business finance is an invaluable asset. So, let's dive in and decode the financial lexicon together!

# Understanding Financial Basics

For many, finance may seem like an intricate and convoluted field, layered with complex jargon and intricate calculations. However, at its core, finance is fundamentally about understanding how money works within a business, how it's earned, managed, and how it grows.

1. **Revenue, Profit, and Loss:** Revenue represents the total amount of money a business generates from its operations. It's the lifeline that fuels a company's growth and operations. Profit is what remains after subtracting all the costs and expenses from the revenue. If expenses exceed revenue, a business experiences a loss. Understanding these concepts is essential to grasp the financial health of a business.

2. **Assets and Liabilities:** Assets are resources that a business owns and can use to generate income, like inventory, machinery, property, or cash. Liabilities are financial obligations or debts that a business needs to settle, such as loans, unpaid bills, or salaries. The difference between total assets and total liabilities represents a business's net worth or equity.

3. **Cash Flow:** Cash flow refers to the movement of cash into and out of a business. Positive cash flow means a business is generating more cash than it's spending, while negative cash flow indicates the opposite. Monitoring cash flow is vital for ensuring a business has enough liquidity for its operations and growth.

4. **Cost of Goods Sold (COGS) and Operating Expenses:** COGS represents the direct costs incurred to produce the goods or services a company sells. It includes material costs and direct labor costs. Operating expenses, on the other hand, are the costs

associated with running the business, excluding direct production costs. These include rent, utilities, salaries, marketing costs, etc.

5. **Capital and Capital Structure:** Capital refers to the financial resources a business uses to fund its operations and growth. It can come from equity (ownership) or debt. A company's capital structure is the mix of debt and equity financing it uses.

6. **Return on Investment (ROI):** ROI measures the profitability of an investment. It's calculated by dividing the net profit from an investment by the cost of the investment. The higher the ROI, the more profitable the investment.

Understanding these financial basics is the first step in mastering the language of business. With a strong foundation, entrepreneurs can make more informed decisions, plan effectively, and communicate clearly about their business's financial status and needs. Remember, the key to effective financial management is not just about making money, but also wisely managing and growing it.

## Navigating Financial Challenges

Running a business is like sailing a ship in a sea filled with storms and calm waters alike. Entrepreneurs often have to navigate a multitude of financial challenges to ensure the survival and growth of their businesses. Here, we shed light on common financial hurdles and how to overcome them:

1. **Cash Flow Management:** Maintaining a positive cash flow can be challenging, especially for startups and small businesses. Entrepreneurs should regularly monitor their cash inflows and outflows, cut unnecessary expenses, streamline operations, and ensure they have a cash reserve for emergencies.

2. **Access to Capital:** Acquiring capital to fund business operations or expansions is another common challenge. Entrepreneurs can address this by exploring various financing options such as traditional loans, venture capital, crowdfunding, or angel investment. Also, creating a solid business plan can help attract potential investors.

3. **Managing Debt:** While loans can provide necessary capital, excessive debt can cripple a business. Entrepreneurs should develop a strategic plan for debt repayment, negotiate favorable terms with lenders, and avoid unnecessary borrowing.

4. **Financial Planning and Forecasting:** Anticipating future expenses and revenues is crucial for strategic planning. Entrepreneurs should regularly perform financial forecasting, take into account industry trends, and adjust plans as necessary.

5. **Compliance with Regulations:** Businesses must comply with a variety of financial regulations and standards, which can be complex. Hiring a

professional accountant or financial advisor can help ensure compliance and avoid potential penalties.

6. **Financial Risk Management:** Entrepreneurs must identify potential financial risks and take measures to mitigate them. This may involve diversifying revenue sources, purchasing insurance, and implementing robust financial controls.

7. **Pricing Strategy:** Setting the right price for products or services is crucial for profitability but can be tricky. Entrepreneurs need to understand their market, competition, cost structure, and value proposition to set effective prices.

Overcoming these financial challenges requires a combination of knowledge, strategy, and adaptability. By understanding these issues and implementing proactive measures, entrepreneurs can safeguard their businesses from potential financial pitfalls and set the stage for sustainable growth.

# Financial Planning and Budgeting

If running a business is a voyage, then financial planning and budgeting is the map that helps entrepreneurs navigate the choppy waters of the enterprise. This process not only informs the decision-making process but also allows for greater control over the financial health and future of your venture. Let's dig deeper into these indispensable tools.

1. **Understanding Financial Planning:** Financial planning is the process of mapping out a business's financial goals and developing strategies to achieve them. This process typically considers the company's current financial situation, growth objectives, and risk tolerance. It encompasses various aspects such as revenue projection, cost estimation, capital requirement, and profitability analysis.

2. **The Need for a Budget:** A budget serves as a financial guide for businesses. It outlines where money will come from and how it will be spent over a specified period. Budgets help entrepreneurs allocate resources efficiently, monitor performance, identify financial trends, manage cash flow, and ensure that the business stays on track to achieve its financial goals.

3. **Developing a Budget:** Budget development involves estimating future income and expenses based on past data, current market trends, and strategic plans. It requires a clear understanding of your business model, operating costs, revenue sources, and potential financial risks. Your budget should be realistic, flexible, and aligned with your business strategy.

4. **Monitoring and Adjusting the Budget:** Regularly reviewing and updating the budget is crucial. It allows entrepreneurs to compare actual performance against

planned objectives, identify any discrepancies, and adjust accordingly. If revenue falls short or expenses are higher than anticipated, immediate action can be taken to prevent financial strain.

5. **Long-term Financial Planning:** While budgeting typically focuses on the short term, financial planning looks at the long term. It involves projecting future financial trends, planning for major expenditures, anticipating financial challenges, and preparing for various business scenarios. Long-term financial planning helps entrepreneurs guide their businesses toward sustained profitability and growth.

6. **Leveraging Financial Software:** Today, various financial software tools can assist with budgeting and planning. These tools can automate calculations, generate insightful reports, track performance in real time, and simplify financial management.

Remember, financial planning and budgeting is not a one-time task, but an ongoing process that should evolve with your business. With careful planning and disciplined budgeting, entrepreneurs can create a solid financial foundation for their ventures, positioning them for success in the competitive business landscape.

## Decoding Financial Reports

Financial reports serve as a business's report card, revealing its financial health and performance. They are essential for making informed business decisions, attracting investors, obtaining loans, and ensuring legal compliance. To an untrained eye, these reports can seem overwhelming with their array of numbers and financial jargon. But with a little guidance, you can learn to decode them. Here's how:

1. **Understanding the Balance Sheet:** The balance sheet provides a snapshot of a business's financial position at a specific point in time. It lists the company's assets (what it owns), liabilities (what it owes), and equity (the owner's share). The fundamental equation of the balance sheet is Assets = Liabilities + Equity. Understanding the balance sheet helps gauge a company's liquidity, solvency, and risk level.

2. **Deciphering the Income Statement:** The income statement, also known as the profit and loss statement, shows a company's profitability over a specific period. It details the revenue earned, expenses incurred, and the resulting net income or loss. Analyzing an income statement helps track revenues and costs, measure profitability, and understand the company's earning capacity.

3. **Interpreting the Cash Flow Statement:** The cash flow statement outlines the cash generated and used in operating, investing, and financing activities over a period. It helps entrepreneurs understand how cash is moving in and out of the business, giving insights into liquidity and the company's ability to cover short-term obligations.

4. **Analyzing Financial Ratios:** Financial ratios are

mathematical calculations using figures from financial statements. They help in understanding a company's profitability, efficiency, liquidity, solvency, and market value. Some key ratios include the debt-to-equity ratio (financial risk), current ratio (short-term liquidity), gross profit margin (profitability), and return on assets (efficiency).

5. **Appreciating the Notes to Accounts:** These notes provide additional information about the figures in the financial statements, offering a clearer picture of a company's financial status. They may include details on accounting methods, commitments, contingencies, and a breakdown of specific items.

6. **Utilizing Financial Software:** Many software tools can help generate and analyze financial reports, making the process easier and more accessible. They offer visual representations of data, trend analyses, ratio calculations, and more.

Understanding financial reports is a crucial skill for any entrepreneur. It provides insights into a company's past performance, present condition, and prospects. While learning to decode these reports may seem daunting, doing so can empower you to make smarter business decisions, leading your venture toward sustained success.

# CHAPTER 13: NETWORKING: THE POWER OF CONNECTIONS

In the world of entrepreneurship, where you're going matters a great deal, but who you journey with can make all the difference. This metaphorical voyage encapsulates the essence of our thirteenth chapter, "Networking: The Power of Connections."

Networking, at its core, is about cultivating and nurturing relationships that can facilitate both personal and professional growth. These relationships could be with mentors, peers, investors, customers, suppliers, or even competitors. The value of a solid network is often underestimated in the entrepreneurial journey. Still, it's an indisputable fact that having a robust network can open doors to opportunities you may never have imagined.

In this chapter, we'll demystify the art and science of networking, revealing why it's so vital for entrepreneurs and how it can be harnessed effectively. We'll delve into various aspects of networking, from making a great first impression to maintaining long-lasting, fruitful connections. You'll discover that networking isn't merely about trading business cards at conferences, but about building and sustaining relationships based on mutual respect and benefit.

We'll explore the different types of networks and their relevance to your entrepreneurial journey. You'll learn how to navigate networking events, leverage social media for networking, and even master the art of 'elevator pitches.' Also, we'll uncover how you can become a resource for your network, thus enhancing your value and credibility.

So, gear up to unlock the power of connections. Remember, in the world of business, it's often not just about what you know, but who you know. As you journey through this chapter, you may find insights and strategies that help you build a network that propels you and your business toward unprecedented success.

## The Art of Building Connections

When it comes to entrepreneurship, building connections isn't merely an option; it's a necessity. But it isn't as simple as just meeting people and exchanging contact information. The art of building connections goes deeper, reaching into the realm of genuine human interaction, mutual respect, and shared value. In this sub-chapter, we delve into the nuts and bolts of establishing and nurturing valuable connections.

Let's start with the first step—meeting new people. In a world where digital interactions often replace face-to-face encounters, various platforms offer networking opportunities. From social media networks to professional networking platforms, online forums, and webinars, the digital world is ripe with potential contacts. But remember, the key isn't just to add people to your contact list; it's to forge connections with those who can add value to your journey and vice versa.

Approach new interactions with curiosity. Show interest in the other person's work, ideas, and experiences. When you show sincere interest, it not only helps you understand their needs better but also makes the other person feel valued—a critical step in establishing a genuine connection.

Next, effective communication is essential. Remember, communication isn't just about speaking; it's equally about listening. Practice active listening. When people feel heard and understood, they are more likely to open up, trust you, and reciprocate your interest.

Then, identify the mutual benefits. A strong connection is one that both parties stand to gain. This could be in the form of knowledge, resources, opportunities, or support. Highlight what you bring to the table and understand what they can offer. This mutual exchange fosters a relationship based on value, increasing its longevity and depth.

Lastly, consistency is key. Building connections is not a one-time activity, but a process. Keep in touch with your contacts, provide updates about your work, ask about theirs, and offer help when you can. Show them that you are not just interested in a transactional relationship but genuinely value the connection.

In essence, the art of building connections is about authenticity, effective communication, and mutual value. As an entrepreneur, mastering this art can open doors to numerous opportunities, making your journey to success smoother and more enriching.

## *Effectively Utilizing Social Platforms*

In the digital era, social platforms have emerged as powerful tools for networking. They offer opportunities to connect with a global audience, access diverse viewpoints, collaborate, and broaden your entrepreneurial horizons. Yet, merely having a profile on these platforms isn't enough. The key lies in using them effectively. This sub-chapter will guide you on how to harness the power of social platforms to nurture your entrepreneurial network.

The first step is to choose the right platforms. While it might be tempting to create a profile on every available platform, it's crucial to choose those that align with your business goals. LinkedIn, for instance, is excellent for professional networking, while Instagram or Pinterest might be more suitable for a visually oriented-business.

Once you've chosen your platforms, ensure that your profiles represent you and your venture accurately and professionally. Your profiles are your digital business cards. A well-crafted profile with a professional photo, a clear description of what you do, and a showcase of your achievements can attract the right connections.

Content creation is another powerful strategy. By regularly sharing valuable content related to your business or industry, you position yourself as a thought leader, attract like-minded individuals, and increase visibility. This could be in the form of blog posts, infographics, webinars, or simple status updates.

Engaging with others is equally important. Don't just broadcast your message; involve others in a conversation. Respond to comments, participate in relevant discussions, and share others' content that aligns with your values. This interaction creates a two-way dialogue, fosters relationships, and enhances your online presence.

Remember to leverage the power of groups and communities. These are spaces where like-minded individuals gather, making them ideal for targeted networking. Participate actively in these groups, share your insights, ask questions, and offer assistance. Over time, these interactions can lead to meaningful connections.

Lastly, treat online connections with the same professionalism as offline ones. Be respectful, keep your commitments, and remember that every interaction contributes to your brand.

Navigating social platforms for networking might seem daunting, but with the right approach, these digital spaces can become invaluable assets in your entrepreneurial journey. Remember, it's not about the quantity of connections but the quality. Be strategic, be consistent, and you'll soon see your network thrive.

# Maintaining Professional Relationships

Creating connections is only the first step in the networking process. Once you've established these relationships, you need to put in the effort to maintain and nurture them. The real value of networking comes from the long-term relationships that you build, and this sub-chapter will provide you with insights on how to maintain these professional relationships.

The foundation of any relationship lies in mutual respect and understanding. This is particularly true for professional relationships where each party has distinct goals and interests. Always respect the other person's time, viewpoint, and professional boundaries. Understanding and acknowledging these aspects is crucial for a sustainable professional relationship.

Communication is the lifeblood of relationships. Stay in touch with your contacts regularly, not just when you need something. Share updates about your business, congratulate them on their achievements, or just send a note to check-in. The aim is to keep the lines of communication open and the relationship active.

Professional relationships are not just about taking but also about giving. Look for ways you can add value to your contacts. This could be in the form of sharing a useful resource, providing a business referral, or offering your expertise in a specific area. When you help others, they are more likely to reciprocate, thus strengthening the relationship.

One important aspect of maintaining relationships is managing and resolving conflicts professionally. Disagreements are inevitable, but the way you handle them can make a big difference. Be open to feedback, handle disagreements with diplomacy, and strive for solutions that are beneficial for all parties involved.

Attend industry events, conferences, and seminars. These not only provide learning opportunities but also allow you to meet your contacts in person, fostering stronger relationships. If physical meetings are not possible, consider virtual meetups.

Finally, remember that maintaining professional relationships takes time and effort. Not every contact will evolve into a strong relationship, and that's okay. Focus your energies on relationships that are mutually beneficial and align with your professional goals.

In the entrepreneurial world, your network can be one of your greatest assets. By learning to maintain your professional relationships effectively, you'll have a robust network that supports your entrepreneurial journey and contributes to your success.

## The Power of Collaboration

Collaboration is a potent tool in the hands of an entrepreneur. By working together with others, whether they are within your organization or outside, you unlock a wellspring of creative energy, different perspectives, and diversified skills. This sub-chapter is dedicated to exploring the power of collaboration and the ways it can propel your entrepreneurial success.

The first point to understand is that collaboration does not dilute individual brilliance. Instead, it amplifies it. When we pool our abilities and work toward a common goal, the result is often more than the sum of its parts. Each person brings their unique strengths to the table, allowing for a more comprehensive approach to problem-solving.

Collaboration often leads to innovation. The sharing of ideas and knowledge encourages creative thinking and can spark new ideas that would not have occurred in isolation. This innovative power of collaboration can help you stay competitive and maintain your business's relevance in a rapidly changing market.

Effective collaboration also promotes efficiency. By sharing the workload, tasks can be accomplished more quickly. Additionally, collaboration can minimize errors as multiple people review and refine the work. This can lead to higher productivity and better results for your business.

Moreover, collaboration is a powerful learning tool. It provides an opportunity for team members to learn from each other's experiences and skills. This continuous learning and improvement culture can enhance your team's overall competence, making your business more robust and resilient.

Building and maintaining strong relationships is a crucial

element of successful collaboration. It requires open communication, trust, respect for diversity, and the willingness to compromise. Encouraging these values within your team can foster a collaborative environment that fuels collective success.

However, collaboration does not mean there is no place for leadership. On the contrary, effective leadership is critical to guide the collaborative process and ensure that everyone's efforts are aligned with the organization's goals.

In the entrepreneurial journey, the ability to collaborate effectively can be a game-changer. It can help you tap into a broader pool of skills, spur innovation, increase efficiency, and promote a learning culture—all of which are key ingredients for business success. Therefore, harness the power of collaboration to drive your entrepreneurial endeavors to new heights.

# CHAPTER 14:
# ETHICAL BUSINESS:
# BUILDING TRUST
# AND REPUTATION
# - INTRODUCTION

As we delve deeper into the mind and heart of an entrepreneur, we must discuss a vital aspect that can make or break a business - ethics. No entrepreneur can survive in the long run without a strong moral compass guiding their decisions and actions. This chapter, "Ethical Business: Building Trust and Reputation," explores the crucial role of ethics in entrepreneurship, its direct link to the building of trust, and the subsequent creation of a solid reputation in the marketplace.

In the age of information, transparency has become the norm. Consumers today are more knowledgeable and aware than ever, and they place a high value on ethical business practices. They seek out companies that not only provide a valuable product or service but also align with their values and contribute positively to society. Therefore, embedding ethical considerations into your business strategies is not only morally right but also makes good business sense.

This chapter takes a deep dive into the components of ethical business, outlining why it is an indispensable aspect of successful entrepreneurship. We will explore the various dimensions of ethical conduct, how it contributes to building trust with stakeholders, and why it is a critical element in cultivating a strong business reputation.

Remember, an entrepreneur's success is not merely measured in terms of monetary gains but also terms of the trust and respect earned from customers, employees, partners, and society at large. As we navigate through this chapter, we aim to empower you with the understanding and tools to lead your business with integrity, fairness, and respect.

Ethics, trust, and reputation are intricately woven together in the fabric of a successful business. As an entrepreneur, you have the opportunity to weave a unique pattern that reflects your values, beliefs, and commitment to making a positive impact. Let's embark on this journey of building an ethical business, fostering trust, and enhancing your reputation in the ever-competitive business landscape.

## The Importance of Ethics in Business

The concept of ethics goes far beyond mere legality and encompasses a vast range of moral principles and values that guide our behavior. In the business context, ethics refers to the code of conduct or principles that a company adheres to in its operations. It is the compass that guides decision-making, shapes company culture, and determines the business's impact on its stakeholders and society at large.

So, why is ethics so important in business?

Firstly, ethical business practices foster trust and build a reputation. When a company acts ethically, it sends a powerful message to its customers, employees, partners, and investors. It communicates that the company values fairness, honesty, and integrity over short-term gains. This helps build a level of trust and loyalty that can be the bedrock for long-term success.

Secondly, ethics help in risk mitigation. Ethical considerations can help a company avoid scandals, legal trouble, and the associated financial and reputational risks. By ensuring that all operations are carried out ethically, a company can preemptively address potential issues and safeguard itself from harmful repercussions.

Thirdly, ethics attract talent and investors. In the modern business world, top talents and conscious investors are increasingly drawn toward ethically sound companies. They prefer to align with businesses that mirror their values and are committed to doing what's right.

Moreover, ethics contribute to customer satisfaction.

Consumers today are more conscious about their choices. They prefer businesses that are responsible, transparent, and fair in their dealings. Therefore, maintaining high ethical standards can help attract and retain a strong customer base.

Lastly, ethical businesses tend to be more profitable in the long run. While unethical practices might promise quick, short-term gains, they often lead to detrimental long-term consequences. In contrast, businesses that operate ethically build sustainable relationships with customers, employees, and partners, resulting in sustained growth and profitability.

In essence, the importance of ethics in business is multi-dimensional. It helps create a positive work environment, build strong customer relationships, attract investment, and foster long-term profitability. Above all, it ensures that the business contributes positively to society and leaves a legacy that extends beyond profits. As an entrepreneur, embedding ethics in your business practices is not just the right thing to do, but also a strategic choice for lasting success.

Trust is the cornerstone of any successful business, and building a trustworthy brand is an investment that yields substantial returns. When your brand is trusted, customers are not just loyal; they become brand ambassadors who willingly spread the word about your products or services. But how do you build a trustworthy brand?

**Integrity and Consistency**

The first step toward building a trustworthy brand is to operate with integrity. This means being honest and transparent in all your dealings - with customers, employees, partners, and even competitors. Make sure that your business practices reflect the values and principles you espouse.

Equally important is consistency. Consistency in quality, service, communication, and behavior builds predictability. When customers know what to expect and their experiences align with their expectations, trust naturally follows.

**Effective Communication**

Open and clear communication is key to building trust. Regularly communicate with your customers through various channels. Keep them updated about new products, changes, achievements, and even setbacks. Address their concerns promptly and politely. Admit mistakes when they occur and communicate your plans for rectification. Honesty in communication not only builds trust but also fosters respect.

**Quality Products and Services**

No amount of marketing or communication can substitute for the quality of your products or services. Make sure what you offer meets or exceeds industry standards and delivers on the promises made. When customers are satisfied with the quality of your products or services, they are more likely to trust your brand.

## Customer-Centric Approach

A customer-centric approach can also help build trust. Listen to your customers, value their feedback, and make changes accordingly. When customers feel heard and valued, they are more likely to trust your brand.

## Social Proof

Leverage the power of social proof to build trust. Showcase testimonials and reviews from satisfied customers. Highlight your associations with trusted entities. Awards, recognitions, and endorsements can also enhance your brand's trustworthiness.

## Ethical Advertising

Avoid deceptive advertising practices. Make sure your ads accurately represent your products or services. Misleading ads might help you make a sale, but they will damage your reputation and customer trust in the long run.

In conclusion, building a trustworthy brand requires a strategic, long-term approach. It's about delivering value consistently, communicating effectively, respecting your customers, and always upholding your ethical standards. When done right, it can set your brand apart and provide a solid foundation for lasting success.

In the dynamic landscape of business, ethical dilemmas are inevitable. These are complex situations where you're faced with difficult choices, each carrying potential for both risk and reward. Successfully navigating these ethical dilemmas is key to maintaining a positive reputation and promoting a healthy business environment. Here's how you can navigate ethical dilemmas effectively:

## 1. Recognize the Ethical Issue

The first step in navigating an ethical dilemma is recognizing that it exists. An ethical issue typically arises when a situation requires you to choose between two or more alternatives that may seem equally valid but have different ethical implications. It's important to be aware of the values and principles at stake and understand how your decision could impact them.

## 2. Gather Information

Once you've identified an ethical dilemma, gather as much information as possible. Understand the facts, evaluate the potential outcomes, and consider the viewpoints of all parties involved. Remember, the more information you have, the better equipped you'll be to make an informed decision.

## 3. Evaluate Your Options

Evaluate each potential course of action objectively. Consider the ethical implications of each option and how they align with your business's values and principles. Think about the potential consequences of each decision, both immediate and long-term.

## 4. Seek Advice

Don't hesitate to seek advice when faced with an ethical dilemma. This could be from mentors, business partners, or other trusted individuals who can offer a different perspective. They can help you understand the issue better and may offer valuable insights that you might have overlooked.

## 5. Make the Decision

Once you've evaluated all your options, make the decision. Remember, there's rarely a perfect solution in an ethical dilemma, but the best decision is usually the one that aligns most closely with your business's values and principles.

## 6. Reflect on the Outcome

After making the decision, take the time to reflect on the outcome. Did it align with your expectations? Did it uphold your business's values and principles? Use this reflection as a learning experience to navigate future ethical dilemmas.

Navigating ethical dilemmas is challenging, but with careful evaluation and thoughtful decision-making, you can uphold your business's integrity and build trust among stakeholders. Remember, the way you handle these dilemmas can significantly impact your business's reputation, so it's essential to approach them with care and transparency.

# Promoting Transparency and Accountability

As we progress in our entrepreneurial journey, it's crucial to understand the value of two core principles: transparency and accountability. These twin pillars are essential to fostering trust with employees, partners, investors, and customers. They also serve as critical underpinnings to maintaining ethical standards in your business.

## 1. Understanding Transparency

Transparency means being open, clear, and straightforward about your business operations and decisions. It involves making information accessible to stakeholders, enabling them to understand the 'why' behind your actions. Whether it's financial data, business strategies, or decision-making processes, sharing this information can build trust and credibility for your brand.

## 2. Encouraging Accountability

Accountability refers to taking responsibility for one's actions. In a business context, this means holding oneself and others answerable for the decisions made and actions taken. By promoting a culture of accountability, businesses can encourage employees to take ownership of their tasks and be responsible for their outcomes, fostering a sense of integrity and commitment within the organization.

**Promoting Transparency:**

Promoting transparency starts from the top. As a leader, be open about your strategies, objectives, and expectations. Share key metrics with your team and stakeholders. Embrace open dialogue, inviting feedback and ideas. Transparency also means acknowledging mistakes and failures - seeing them as opportunities to learn and improve.

A critical aspect of promoting transparency is clear, open communication. Make sure information is disseminated accurately and promptly to avoid misinformation. Utilize technology to your advantage - digital platforms can help keep stakeholders informed about important updates and developments.

**Fostering Accountability:**

To foster accountability, set clear expectations for every team member, along with corresponding responsibilities. Ensure that everyone understands their roles and the impact of their actions on the overall objectives of the business.

Develop a system for tracking performance and progress. Regular evaluations can help identify areas of improvement and offer opportunities to recognize and reward responsible behavior.

Encourage an environment where employees feel safe to admit mistakes. Instead of promoting a blame culture, focus on learning from these situations. When mistakes are made, help your team understand the consequences and work collectively toward a solution.

Finally, lead by example. Show your team that you're not just a title leader but also in action. Demonstrate that you're accountable for your decisions and actions, setting a precedent for the rest of the team to follow.

Promoting transparency and fostering accountability not only helps in ethical business conduct but also drives performance and productivity. They create a culture of trust and respect, where everyone feels valued, leading to a more committed, motivated, and effective workforce.

# CHAPTER 15: LIFE-WORK BALANCE: THE ULTIMATE ENTREPRENEURIAL CHALLENGE

Every entrepreneur's journey is a vibrant tapestry of passion, determination, and relentless drive for success. Yet, this beautiful tapestry can become frayed at the edges if not meticulously woven with threads of balance. It's a delicate dance, the art of maintaining equilibrium between the demanding business world and the personal realm, where time is often the most sought-after currency. As we venture into the final chapter of this book, we'll explore the concept of life-work balance and its pivotal role in the entrepreneurial landscape.

A life tilted heavily toward work may breed professional success, but it often comes at the cost of personal happiness and well-being. Similarly, an overly personal life may create a comfortable bubble, albeit one that restrains entrepreneurial growth. So, how can one strike a balance? Is it possible to thrive in both arenas without sacrificing the other? These are the questions we will unravel in this chapter.

Here, we will dive into the essential strategies to manage your time efficiently, maintain your health and well-being, foster meaningful relationships, and still achieve your entrepreneurial goals. This isn't about setting strict boundaries between your work and personal life, but rather about integrating them harmoniously, and yes, it's a challenge. But it's one well worth embracing as it shapes you not only into a successful entrepreneur but also a fulfilled individual.

Welcome to the ultimate entrepreneurial challenge - attaining a life-work balance. Buckle up, for it's time to learn, introspect, and find the rhythm that best resonates with your entrepreneurial spirit and personal life.

# Understanding the Concept of Balance

The term 'balance' often conjures up an image of a scale where equal weights are placed on each side, maintaining a perfect equilibrium. However, when applied to life and work, the concept transcends this simplistic analogy. Life-work balance isn't about splitting your time evenly between personal and professional endeavors. Instead, it's about effectively managing your roles and responsibilities in such a way that neither your happiness nor your business success has to be compromised.

Let's begin by debunking a popular myth: life-work balance is not a fixed state of equilibrium. The balance is dynamic, ever-changing, and as unique as the individuals themselves. What works for one person might not work for another. Some might thrive in high-pressure work environments, finding the very chaos exhilarating and invigorating, while others may require a more serene, relaxed setting to give their best.

Moreover, the balance is not always 50-50, and it doesn't need to be. There might be times when your business needs more attention - during a product launch, a crisis, or an expansion, for instance. Similarly, there will be periods when your personal life calls for more focus - family emergencies, health issues, or personal commitments.

Understanding balance in the life-work context means recognizing that it's okay for the scales to tip from one side to the other occasionally. It's about finding your unique equilibrium, which allows you to meet both professional and personal demands without sacrificing your well-being. It's about being in control of your time and energy, knowing when to engage and when to disengage.

This balance does not just contribute to individual well-being, but it also has profound implications for business success. An entrepreneur who masters the art of balance is more likely to be a focused, creative, and effective leader, one who leads by example, promotes a healthy work culture, and thus drives their enterprise toward success. As we navigate through the intricacies of life-work balance in this chapter, remember, balance is not a destination, but a journey of continuous adaptation and adjustment.

## Setting Boundaries

Life, in many ways, resembles a canvas where different areas represent different aspects of our existence – work, family, friends, health, hobbies, personal growth, and so forth. As an entrepreneur, it is often challenging to prevent the colors from one area bleeding into the others, thereby disturbing the overall harmony of the canvas. This is where the concept of 'boundaries' comes into play.

Boundaries, both physical and psychological, act as barriers that help maintain a distinct separation between different areas of life. They are essential rules or limits that a person establishes to identify reasonable, safe, and permissible ways to behave toward them and how they will respond when someone oversteps these limits. In the context of life-work balance, boundaries can be seen as tools that protect your personal space and time, prevent burnout, and ensure that work stress doesn't spill over into your personal life.

Setting boundaries involves clearly defining your availability and expectations, both for yourself and others. It's about communicating with your team when you are accessible for work discussions and when you wish to focus on your personal life. It also entails setting limits on how much time you spend working after regular hours or during the weekend.

However, establishing boundaries is not enough. You need to respect and uphold these limits to make them effective. This might mean resisting the urge to check your email during family dinner, turning off work-related notifications after a certain hour, or saying no to commitments that infringe upon your time.

Remember, setting boundaries doesn't make you less dedicated or passionate about your business. Instead, it reflects your commitment to maintaining your mental and emotional health, which is vital for long-term success and productivity. By setting and maintaining boundaries, you not only ensure your time is respected but also set a powerful example for your team, promoting a healthier and more respectful work culture.

Throughout this chapter, we'll explore how you can set, communicate, and maintain these boundaries effectively, helping you to nurture a healthy life-work balance and enhance both your personal well-being and business success.

## Prioritizing Health and Well-being

Entrepreneurship can be a consuming endeavor. The thrill of building something from the ground up, the drive to make a difference, and the continuous quest for success can often lead entrepreneurs to put their health and well-being on the back burner. Yet, as counterintuitive as it might seem, this approach can be detrimental to both personal life and business growth. In this sub-chapter, we underscore the importance of prioritizing health and well-being as an integral part of achieving a life-work balance.

In the quest to achieve entrepreneurial success, it is vital to understand that you, as the leader, are your business's most valuable asset. Like any precious resource, you must maintain and care for your health to ensure that you can perform at your best. This includes physical health—maintaining a balanced diet, ensuring regular exercise, getting adequate sleep—as well as mental health—managing stress, practicing mindfulness, and seeking support when needed.

However, prioritizing health is not just about avoiding illness or burnout. It is about cultivating a state of complete physical, mental, and social well-being that enables you to enjoy a high quality of life and contribute your best to your business. It means creating a lifestyle that supports and enhances your ability to cope with stress and bounce back from adversities.

Importantly, health and well-being should not be viewed as something 'extra' you do outside of work. Instead, they need to be integrated into your daily routines and your business culture. This could include measures like setting aside time for regular breaks during work, promoting a culture of openness about mental health in the workplace, providing health-friendly options in the workplace, or encouraging regular team activities that promote physical health and team bonding.

Prioritizing your health and well-being sets the foundation for sustainable productivity and success. It is an investment that not only benefits you personally but also has far-reaching implications for your team's morale, your business's culture, and ultimately, its performance.

As we delve deeper into this sub-chapter, we will provide practical strategies for integrating health and well-being into your entrepreneurial journey, demonstrating that a healthy entrepreneur is indeed a more successful entrepreneur.

## Achieving Fulfillment:
## Beyond Success

Success, as defined by many, often revolves around achieving business objectives, scaling operations, and making profits. While these are essential aspects of entrepreneurship, they are not the only determinants of a fulfilled life. In this sub-chapter, we delve into the concept of fulfillment and explore how it extends beyond the traditional definition of success.

Fulfillment is a deeply personal and profoundly powerful concept. It encompasses a sense of satisfaction and happiness derived not just from achieving goals, but also from the journey toward these achievements. For an entrepreneur, fulfillment can be about making a positive impact, pursuing a passion, living in alignment with personal values, or fostering a nurturing work environment for a team.

However, achieving fulfillment does not happen automatically upon reaching certain business milestones. It is a continuous process that requires introspection and mindful action. It is about aligning your entrepreneurial journey with what genuinely matters to you. This might mean prioritizing certain aspects of life—like family, health, or personal growth—alongside your business goals.

Part of achieving fulfillment also involves cultivating gratitude and appreciating the journey as much as the destination. Recognizing the small victories, celebrating progress, and valuing the process can imbue your entrepreneurial journey with a sense of fulfillment that is enduring and deeply satisfying.

Additionally, entrepreneurs who seek fulfillment tend to create businesses that reflect their values and passions, leading to organizations that inspire, motivate, and make a positive impact. These businesses often go beyond being just profit-making entities to becoming platforms that enrich lives, communities, and environments.

In this sub-chapter, we will guide you through practical strategies to seek and achieve fulfillment in your entrepreneurial journey. We'll delve into various facets of fulfillment, ranging from defining what it means to you, to integrating it into your entrepreneurial ethos, to using it as a compass to navigate the entrepreneurial landscape. The pursuit of fulfillment, we will discover, goes hand in hand with achieving a balanced life and sustained entrepreneurial success.

# CONCLUSION: THE ENTREPRENEURIAL JOURNEY AND BEYOND

As we close the pages of this book, it is essential to remember that the entrepreneurial journey, as we have explored, is much more than a simple path from idea generation to commercial success. It is a life-long learning process, a delicate dance of passion and pragmatism, a continuous adjustment to evolving circumstances, and above all, a deeply personal and transformative journey.

We have traversed together through the various facets of entrepreneurship, from the birth of an idea to the complex world of financial acumen. We've considered the crucial importance of leadership, emotional intelligence, and innovation in an ever-changing business landscape. We have also underscored the significance of resilience, risk-taking, and persistence in the face of daunting challenges.

At the heart of our exploration lies the fundamental understanding that success is a multifaceted construct, transcending the narrow confines of profit and loss. The pillars of ethical business, the power of networking, and the challenging yet rewarding task of achieving a life-work balance constitute vital components of the entrepreneurial journey.

Embracing failure as a teacher, leveraging passion as the driving force, and harnessing the power of decision-making are key lessons we have unearthed. These insights serve as powerful tools in your entrepreneurial arsenal, guiding you through the complex labyrinth of business ventures.

Remember, there is no 'one-size-fits-all' approach to entrepreneurship. Your journey will be as unique as you are. And while this book provides a guide, the real map lies within you. Your values, your passion, your vision, and your spirit are the true compass guiding your entrepreneurial journey.

As you step forward into your entrepreneurial journey, or as you continue on the path you've already embarked on, keep these insights close. Draw from their strength, wisdom, and encouragement. But, most importantly, don't forget to enjoy the journey. Entrepreneurship is not just about reaching a destination; it's about growing, learning, and becoming, every step of the way.

The world of entrepreneurship is vibrant and varied, filled with challenges, but also abundant with opportunities. Armed with the tools, insights, and lessons from this book, you are well-equipped to chart your entrepreneurial path. Remember, your journey is uniquely yours, and every challenge, every success, and every failure are a step toward your personal growth and success.

Here's to you, the entrepreneur, and the exciting journey you are about to undertake or are already on. Trust in your capabilities, stay true to your values, and never stop learning. Here's to your success, in all its varied and personal forms. And here's to the impact you will make, the lives you will touch, and the change you will bring to the world. Because, in the end, that's what being an entrepreneur truly means.

Made in United States
North Haven, CT
29 December 2023

46676852R00088